Proverbs of Fire

Proverbial Wisdom
for Single Christian Women

Proverbs of Fire

Proverbial Wisdom
for Single Christian Women

by Tiffany Buckner

Anointed Fire™ House Christian Publishing
www.anointedfirehouse.com

I dedicate this book to its true Author: YAHWEH. May Your Name be glorified throughout this entire book. I love You today and forevermore. ♡

Table of Contents

Introduction

Proverbs of Fire is a powerful collection of quotes and advice that have been written by Tiffany "AnointedFire" Buckner. Some of these powerful messages were shared on social media, while others have never been shared.

This powerful book will encourage you, correct you, and humor you at times. It will also inspire and challenge you, thus helping you to move to new heights in understanding, love and patience.

Proverbs of Fire was birthed after the Holy Spirit instructed author Tiffany Buckner to take many of the messages she's shared online and place them in a book. What resulted was a power-packed and heaven-sent guide filled with more than one thousand quotes, messages and short stories.

Proverbs of Fire is in no way a part of the Bible, nor is it an attempt to redefine the Scriptures. The information contained in this book is simply wise quotes and information shared with and through Kingdom Ambassador, Tiffany Buckner. It is not an extension of the book of Proverbs; it is a devotional style book with quotes that come straight from wisdom's table.

Proverbs of Fire

Chapter 1

Proverb of Fire 1
You can't win a loser.

Proverb of Fire 2
You can't drag anybody closer to God, but you can change your proximity to them.

Proverb of Fire 3
Faith isn't faith until it makes no sense.

Proverb of Fire 4
Sin's orgasm is called death. Don't pleasure sin. You won't like it when it's finished.

Proverb of Fire 5
When people work hard at being "sexy," they end up reaping sex-starved or sex-craved perverts who want to lease their bodies while manipulating their minds.

Proverb of Fire 6
People who don't sow anything are oftentimes the first ones to go out looking for a harvest.

Proverb of Fire 7
Going back and forth with a person who has no understanding is the same as sowing good seeds into bad ground.

Proverb of Fire 8
It is better to self correct than to self destruct.

Proverb of Fire 9
Satan has plans for you, but they don't end with you getting

what you want. They end with you getting what you deserve.

Proverb of Fire 10
God is good at being God, but you are not.

Proverb of Fire 11
If they were to let a prideful man into the control room of a submarine, he'd see a bunch of equipment that he would not understand. Sure, he'd know that the controls and buttons are used to operate the submarine, but he would not understand their functions. If he was hired to work in the control room and really wanted the job, it would be hard for him to admit that he doesn't understand the controls or know what he's doing. So, he'd try to learn by trial and error, hoping that he'll figure things out on his own. Nevertheless, in a submarine, you don't have the luxury of making too many mistakes, therefore, a prideful, needy man would cause a submarine to sink and kill everyone on board. The same thing goes when a man marries a woman he is not ordained to be with. He sees her personality, her character, and her flaws, but he cannot understand them. She's too elaborate for him, so instead of admitting that he cannot operate as her covering, he'll attempt to figure her out through trial and error, but with marriage, one doesn't have the luxury of repeatedly crashing another human being. Sure, there will be some bumps here and there, but the bumps aren't an indication that something's wrong with the submarine; sometimes, the bumps simply mean that the man in the control room does not know what he's doing. The point is— Every woman is a beautiful and elaborate weave of love, designed to represent God's softer side. You don't want to be soft with a man who does not recognize his strength or

understand the complex, but anointed creature that you are. That's why you have to wait for God to send your God-appointed husband to you. No other man will understand your design.

Proverb of Fire 12
You can never get on Satan's good side because he doesn't have one.

Proverb of Fire 13
Make sure the heart of the prophet is as true as the words he or she speaks.

Proverb of Fire 14
Love never fails and lust never wins.

Proverb of Fire 15
You don't belong to yourself so you don't have the right to give you away. Only God does. If you give yourself to the wrong man, you will hand him your flesh, but God will not give him the understanding, wisdom or knowledge he'll need to cover your spirit. This means that your marriage will be flesh-driven until it's driven apart by flesh.

Proverb of Fire 16
God got the last Word in the beginning of time.

Proverb of Fire 17
If the Devil ain't mad at you, he must be proud of you.

Proverb of Fire 18
Sex outside the covenant of marriage isn't just between two people. Believe it or not, every devil involved gets in on the

action.

Proverb of Fire 19
You're either a worrier or a warrior.

Proverb of Fire 20
God has enough servants; He is looking for faithful servants.

Proverb of Fire 21
A rose doesn't need as much water to grow as a tree. In other words, some people get more storms because of the height in the spirit they are called to walk in and the depth of wisdom God is pouring into them. Sure, a rose is pretty to look at, but it doesn't last as long as a tree.

Proverb of Fire 22
You can choose your own spouse or you can wait for the one God chose for you. Look at your track record and ask yourself if you can be trusted to choose your own spouse.

Proverb of Fire 23
Mercy is the leash God has placed on our sins to keep them from paying us what we're truly owed! Grace is God giving us time to get a headstart so that we can run into a building called Repentance; that way, when our sins come looking for us, we won't be found. Foolishness is yanking mercy's chain and taking grace for granted, thinking that you can keep playing with sin. Know this: All God has to do is let your sin off that leash, and it will show you how merciless it is. Repent today because tomorrow is not promised.

Proverb of Fire 24
You can't stand with God and against Him at the same time.

Proverb of Fire 25
Some things aren't lost in translation; they simply fall upon the ears of people who've already prejudged your character.

Proverb of Fire 26
Love has to transcend the love of self before it is made perfect.

Proverb of Fire 27
If God doesn't show up at your wedding, you shouldn't be there either.

Proverb of Fire 28
Shifting is never a comfortable place because when you shift, you are taken outside of your comfort zone and elevated through and to places you've never been before. No one is comfortable in new settings.

Proverb of Fire 29
Having knowledge is good, but applying that knowledge is better.

Proverb of Fire 30
The mindset of a woman is NOT the same as the mindset of a wife. A wife is hidden in God and released to be found by her appointed husband; whereas, a woman is a stray child who'll be picked up by any man who finds her attractive. A man who marries a woman doesn't leave the altar with a wife; he walks away with a married woman!

Proverb of Fire 31
I don't care how old you get, you never stop learning unless you choose to.

Proverb of Fire 32

If the person you call your spiritual covering is in fornication or unrepentant rebellion, please know that you are uncovered! The one thing you don't want is to be struggling in the flesh and not understand why. Whatever's wrong with the head (covering), that is what's wrong with the body (members)! The head can't catch a cold without the whole body being affected!

Proverb of Fire 33

The silliest thing two women can do is fight over a man. The worst thing you can do to a mistress is let her have the cheater she's cheating with full time.

Proverb of Fire 34

People who marry to have legal sex often end up in sexless marriages.

Proverb of Fire 35

You can't live with the Devil Monday through Saturday and then have Sunday sleepovers with God. Choose this day who you will serve.

Proverb of Fire 36

Your sex ain't so good that it can cast out demons or renew minds. If a man is imprisoned by sin, the only thing he can offer you is conjugal visits.

Proverb of Fire 37

If he doesn't have the Holy Spirit, he shouldn't have you.

Proverb of Fire 38

Your faith should have stretch marks.

Proverb of Fire 39
Some folks marry their Goliaths and then spend the rest of their lives trying to overcome them.

Proverb of Fire 40
When you take fornication out of the equation, you are in the same refusing to see your partner through the rose-colored glasses created by the honeymoon stage of unrighteousness. In other words, the two of you REALLY get to know each other, and you can then make a sound decision because you'll be sober enough to hear from God.

Proverb of Fire 41
Yesterday has moved on. Have you?

Proverb of Fire 42
In a debate, a wise man robs himself. He gives away wisdom, but receives empty words in return.

Proverb of Fire 43
You can chop the head off a snake, but that won't change what it is. It'll simply go from being a living snake to a dead snake. You can read the Bible to a pig, but that won't change what it is. It'll simply go from being a regular pig to a legalistic pig because wisdom is too high for it. In other words, stop trying to change people who don't want to be changed and learn to point them in the direction of the God who has the power to change them.

Proverb of Fire 44
Some folks can date for 15 years, get married and then end up divorced. Some folks can court for five days, get married and stay married for 75 years. It's not about how long you

wait; it's about who you wait with and whether God is in it or not.

Proverb of Fire 45
Ahab gave up his inheritance for Jezebel, David's relationship with Bathsheba cost him his son and almost cost him his life, Solomon paid for his many wives with his soul and Samson's marriage to Delilah cost him his freedom, eyesight and his life. There is ALWAYS a price to pay when you loan the anointing to the Devil. Just ask yourself if you're willing to pay it before you dive into it.

Proverb of Fire 46
You can't be the wrong woman complaining because you ended up with the wrong man. Understand the condition of your heart is the direction of your feet.

Proverb of Fire 47
If you hate holiness (and the people who preach it), you hate the Holiest of Holies. If you stone the messenger, it's because you despise the one who sent the message.

Proverb of Fire 48
Whatever it is in your life that you want to die, starve it. Whatever you want to grow, feed it. Stop giving attention to negative things.

Proverb of Fire 49
Frown lines are oftentimes the stretchmarks of bitterness.

Proverb of Fire 50
Never allow yourself to see someone from another person's eyes. You have your own mind for a reason.

Proverb of Fire 51
One sign that you value yourself is your refusal to be mistreated by anyone—high or low, rich or poor, saved or unsaved. Understand this. People are responsible for how they treat you, but you are also responsible for how you allow yourself to be treated. No one can treat you like crap without your permission.

Proverb of Fire 52
The worst marriage one can have is one where the honeymoon ends.

Proverb of Fire 53
You can't talk a devil out of being a devil.

Proverb of Fire 54
There were many words spoken against you, but their words are no match for God's Word. One Word from Him canceled every word curse, lie, and poisonous dart ever sent out against you.

Proverb of Fire 55
There are some people who can pray down heaven, but they can't tap into it. Religiousness is having the image of God, but denying the power thereof.

Proverb of Fire 56
When you say, "I don't understand why he or she acts like that!" or "I don't understand him or her!"—That clearly means you haven't given up anything to understand that person. The Word says that understanding will cost you everything, therefore, to understand me, you have to walk in my shoes, experience my falls, and suffer my losses—To

understand another person, you have to walk in their shoes, experience their falls and suffer their losses.

Dear church: Stop getting mad at folks just because you don't understand them! I used to get mad at people who I didn't understand UNTIL the Lord let me sit in the situations they were sitting in and endure the pains they were enduring —until the Lord let me pay the price for understanding— that's when I learned to shut up and understand that somethings aren't for me to grasp; I only need to know that the wisdom of God is infinite, and He gives me my own portion of it— the portion which He allotted to me—the portion that won't cost me more than I can pay. That's all I need until He gives me more.

Proverb of Fire 57
A man who loves the real you (your eternal being) will not sin against you with fornication. If he tries to lead you into fornication, it is clear that you can't trust his leadership.
Walk away.

Proverb of Fire 58
Taking a devil-filled lover to church won't get him delivered. The Devil has been hanging out at church for a long time.

Proverb of Fire 59
You can't praise your way out of the Devil's bedroom. You have to repent your way out of it.

Proverb of Fire 60
In the dead of winter, we need comforters to cover us and keep us warm. We also need our garments to keep us warm. If we don't cover ourselves in the cold weather, we would

likely die from exposure. How many of you know that God uses the natural things to explain the spiritual things? A soul that has been joined to another person is exposed and needs covering. That's why it's important that the man and woman first have Christ as their covering, and the woman needs her husband to cover her after sex, otherwise, she walks around exposed. All the same, a man who has not accepted Jesus as his Lord and Savior is a man without a covering, and as such, he cannot properly cover a woman; instead, he will expose her. That's why sex has to be had within the confines of a godly marriage where Christ is the head (covering) of the man, and man is the head (covering) of his wife. Ladies, if you let him join himself to you without covering you, whether he's saved or not, you're giving him permission to remove your protective garments, and you can rest assured that the enemy will never miss an opportunity to attack and attach himself to an uncovered woman.

Proverb of Fire 61
Our mindsets are tied to our manifestations; it's similar to "connect-the-dots." What we connect to represents what, or better yet, who we are connected to.

Proverb of Fire 62
A prophet of God who is submitted to a Jezebellic leader often hears from Baal.

Proverb of Fire 63
Everything in the realm of the earth is a response to something. For example, when the enemy attacks you, he is responding to something you did, said, or the call on your life. At the same time, the enemy attacks non-believers just

because they are made in the image of God, and even though they serve him, he still hates them. Everything around you is having a non-verbal conversation with you; for example, when you don't put gas in your car, it responds by not moving. When you eat, your body responds to the food by digesting it. When you speak, the earth responds to the sound of your voice by echoing it. When the wind blows, your hair responds by moving. With that being said, make sure your life is saying the right things so God can respond to you the right way.

Proverb of Fire 64
As believers, our fines tend to be doubled when we know better and still do wrong.

Proverb of Fire 65
You haven't said much until Satan tries to silence you. You haven't done much until Satan tries to stop you.

Proverb of Fire 66
A person will always commit idolatry with themselves before they commit adultery against their spouses.

Proverb of Fire 67
Everything in the realm of the earth has to obey God. Speak the Word to those things, and they'll have to obey you.

Proverb of Fire 68
There will be many people who won't like you for various reasons, but their opinions of you don't matter until they've gotten your attention.

Proverb of Fire 69

The outer adorning of a woman attracts men who walk by sight, but wisdom attracts men of God who walk by faith.

Proverb of Fire 70

Faith is the fuel that will get you to where you're supposed to be, but doubt is a leak in your fuel's tank.

Proverb of Fire 71

Religious people say, "God is still working on me." Godly people say, "Lord, I repent!"

Proverb of Fire 72

Some women entertain Ishmaels while they wait for Isaac, not understanding that those Ishmaels are the reason their Isaacs have been delayed.

Proverb of Fire 73

An unforgiving heart attracts adversaries, but a loving heart attracts friends.

Proverb of Fire 74

Your praises attract blessings. If you rarely praise the Lord, rest assured, your life will reflect that.

Proverb of Fire 75

So many women say, "I slipped up with this guy. It was an accident." That's a well-crafted lie. When I walk, I walk. If I fall down, it wasn't intentional; it was an accident. When I lie down to sleep, my lying down is intentional, and if I stand up, that too was intentional. I can't fall into standing. What's the point? If you have sex with a man you are not married to, your act was intentional unless you were raped. Feeling guilty doesn't mean you didn't intend to lie down and have sex; it simply means that you recognize that what you did was wrong. Serving God is no accident; it has to be done from the heart. Falling into sin is no accident; it is always done from the heart. So what should you do when you fall? Understand that you did not fall when the sin occurred. You were already in iniquity; what was in you simply manifested itself. Now, it's time to take that transgression before the Lord and be delivered from it. Otherwise, you will spend your life at the altar apologizing but not repenting. There is a difference.

Proverb of Fire 76
You are God's private property. Stop letting folks trespass in your life.

Proverb of Fire 77
When you trust that God is going to send you your husband, you will walk by every other man as if you are already a happily married woman. Faith changes the way you walk and think.

Proverb of Fire 78
Asking a pride-filled person to humble him or herself is no different than telling a lion the benefits of being a vegan.

Proverb of Fire 79
So many people look to the stars (horoscopes) when they should be looking to the hills from where their help comes. Horoscopes are ancient Babylonian practices, and as such, are pure and unadulterated witchcraft. When you tap into the powers of divination, you join hands with the Devil, and

he'll use your faith in horoscopes to attack you and your family. Why? Because he hates you. He even hates the people who willfully serve him. Tap into the power of God and let each day play out as it is supposed to play out. Sure, you won't know what tomorrow brings, but that's because you're not supposed to know what tomorrow brings. You're supposed to be walking by faith and not by sight.

Proverb of Fire 80
Your heart is your mouth's birth canal. Whatever you have in your heart will eventually find its way out of your mouth.

Proverb of Fire 81
•The average married couple has sex twice a week; that is, after the honeymoon stage, of course. •The average length of a sexual encounter between a married couple lasts anywhere from two minutes to 20 minutes. (Let's lock in the 20 minute figure to be nice). •There are 10,080 minutes in a week, and the average couple spends 40 of those minutes having sex. This leaves them with 10,040 minutes to figure out if they REALLY like each other outside of the bedroom. (This means the average couple spends less than one percent of their week having sex!) •There are 52 weeks in a year. (This means the average married couple has sex 104 times a year while in the prime of their lives). Of the 365 days in a year, 261 of those days are sexless. What do the numbers tell us? It's simple. Married folks spend more time standing up than they do lying down! That's why it's foolish to marry someone for the sake of fulfilling your sexual appetite. Eight hours of your day will be spent working, and another eight hours will be spent sleeping. You'll spend the majority of the eight hours left cooking, watching television, browsing the

Internet, whooping the kids, talking, resting and making runs. In other words, Hollywood lied! People stay married because they love one another, not because they have sexual chemistry! Marriage isn't one big non-stop romantic event; it is work! That's why you need wisdom, knowledge, patience and understanding before you enter it. Divorce is common because most folks get married trying to pursue the one thing they'll spend the least time doing, and they end up spending the rest of that time looking silly. Don't let mass media seduce you into a union that you don't have the patience to endure or the wisdom to maintain! Wait on God!

Proverb of Fire 82
Every storm you face is an opportunity for greatness.

Proverb of Fire 83
You know you're in a new season when folks from the old season can no longer understand you.

Proverb of Fire 84
Satan is guilty of human trafficking. He sells silly women to foolish men for the price of their souls.

Proverb of Fire 85
To forgive someone is to turn their debts (sins) against you over to the debt collector: YAHWEH. This means they no longer owe you anything, including an apology. Instead, their debt is now to God and He always collects.

Proverb of Fire 86
You have to come outside of yourself to hear from God.

Proverb of Fire 87
Our lives are nothing but a series of choices, and each choice drives us closer to God or closer to death. Go in the righteous direction.

Proverb of Fire 88
Revenge is only sweet when you're bitter.

Proverb of Fire 89
You can't rebuke the Devil if you're sleeping with him.

Proverb of Fire 90
Even though we pray, God isn't as interested in our words as He is with our hearts. The mouth can say whatever the heart bids it to say, but the heart can't lie to God.

Proverb of Fire 91
Lessons learned aren't as powerful as lessons lived.

Proverb of Fire 92
Ladies, pay attention to the type of men who flirt with you. That will help you understand where you are in the Lord. If thugs and rebels are still hissing at you, you need to lay before the cross until whatever they're attracted to falls off you.

Proverb of Fire 93
You can't change the Word of God. The Word of God has to change you.

Proverb of Fire 94
The Devil is a silver-tongued liar. Unfortunately for him, we've got the golden truth on our side.

Proverb of Fire 95
Does the Devil keep coming to your house? Stop inviting him in and make your home an atmosphere of worship daily. Satan is terrified of true godly worship.

Proverb of Fire 96
Sometimes, people aimlessly wait on God to answer questions that He's already answered. Never think that nagging the Lord is gonna wear Him down or you'll end up worn out, held back and still hearing that same "no" that He gave you a year ago.

Proverb of Fire 97
Sin is a foundation that you do not want to build on.

Proverb of Fire 98
YAHWEH is always speaking. You don't need a prophet to hear what He has to say. You simply need to slow down, call on His name and have faith that He will answer you in His time and not yours.

Proverb of Fire 99
Our giving represents our faith, but our taking often represents our fears.

Proverb of Fire 100
Praying for yourself is great, but interceding for others is far more powerful.

Chapter 2

Proverb of Fire 101
What's your reality?

One woman's reality is: She's waiting on God to send her "a" husband.

One woman's reality is: She's waiting on God to save her husband.

One woman's reality is: She's waiting on God to change her husband.

One woman's reality is: She's waiting on God to remove her husband.

One woman's reality is: She's waiting on God to send her "her" already changed husband.

Proverb of Fire 102
You can change the world, but you can't change the Word. You can, however, change the world with the Word.

Proverb of Fire 103
You are designed to win, but broken to fail. Let the Word repair, replenish, and restore you so that you can rise above your present situation.

Proverb of Fire 104
When a fornicator stops fornicating because they want something from God, their abstinence is not counted as their deliverance. Instead, they become dormant fornicators who are trying to manipulate God by giving Him what He requires of them.

Proverb of Fire 105
Your womb is the vault that God wants to send some powerful men and women of God through. The enemy will send his sons to try and access your vault so that he can steal

the treasures of your womb. The pass-code to protect your womb is: purity.

Proverb of Fire 106

An enemy is not a person who opposes you. An enemy is a person who opposes your purpose. Everyone else is just flawed.

Proverb of Fire 107

Some people attempt to fight a battle they can't win against a God who can't lose.

Proverb of Fire 108

Some situations don't require your opinion; they require your prayers.

Proverb of Fire 109

Why is fasting a God idea? Think about trials and tribulations. What exactly do they do? They bring you to the end of yourself, where all that's left for you to do is lean on God. That's what fasting does. It brings you to the end of yourself (no trial needed) so you can depend on God. Sometimes, it comes down to two choices: fast and pray or endure a trial. Either way, when God calls you to come outside of yourself to meet Him, you will have to do just that.

Proverb of Fire 110

Change doesn't happen when Heaven releases what you've been praying for. Change happens when you change your mind about what you already have.

Proverb of Fire 111
We don't just have purpose; we are purpose manifested!

Proverb of Fire 112
A woman is discovered, but a wife is found.

Proverb of Fire 113
A Christian who learns to understand the art of sowing and reaping is a person who has learned to master the wealth of this earth. When you master the wealth, everyone who is mastered by the wealth will build bridges for you to walk on, they will build houses for you to live in, and they will reap up the fruit of the land for you to feast on. Ask God to teach you the principles of sowing and reaping and watch your life change for the better.

Proverb of Fire 114
You are an acquired, unique taste, so tell me why do you get upset when folks don't like you? People collectively like what's common, but only those who can afford different can appreciate different.

Proverb of Fire 115
Never let your flesh tell you that it can sit in the atmosphere of sin and not be moved.

Proverb of Fire 116
Ministry should never be viewed as an opportunity for the minister, but rather an opportunity for those who are ministered to.

Proverb of Fire 117
It is better to confess a sin than it is to be confronted by it.

Proverb of Fire 118

When you're in the season of sowing, you won't see much fruit, but that's because that's your season to give. When you're in the season of reaping, you'll see much fruit, but then, you'll see more opportunities to sow as well. If you learn to watch your seasons, you'll know how to respond to the hardships you face in those seasons; for example, when you sow in tears, you water the harvest and you'll reap in joy. Why is that? Because even though you're faced with opposition, you didn't let your opponent (Satan) change your position, and you kept on sowing! In other words, stop crying and complaining about where you are and sow your way out!

Proverb of Fire 119

Your willingness and desire to obey God builds a bridge between you and heaven.

Proverb of Fire 120

Life is like a school. We are all at some grade level and our desire should be to get promoted, not retained. With that being said, choosing your own guy is like choosing the grade level that's easiest for you and then complaining because you keep finding yourself at the same level with a different teacher.

Proverb of Fire 121

There are many words spoken into the atmosphere, but the Word of God will arrest and cancel out any words that rise up against the Truth.

Proverb of Fire 122

You said, "No weapon formed against me shall prosper!" But

do you know that the man who's trying to get you into fornication is a weapon formed against you? Does the beauty of his face cover the ugliness of his lies so well that you are willing to give up the beauty of holiness just so he can label you as his "girlfriend"? If you've got to fornicate to keep him, that only means that he's on demonic assignment. Stop sleeping with the weapons before they actually do prosper.

Proverb of Fire 123
Say about yourself what God says about you. If you say otherwise, you will have aligned yourself with a lie, and it just may become your reality.

Proverb of Fire 124
The root word of "dismantle" is mantle. Your mantle is your assignment from God, and anyone who comes against that assignment is trying to "dismantle" you. Anyone who does not understand your assignment should not be close enough to you to touch you or your assignment, otherwise, they run the risk of putting their hands or their mouths on the ark of judgment that you are. Israel couldn't let a fool near the ark of the covenant, or he'd touch it and die. Well, that's what happens when you let someone with no vision close to you. They'll put their hands right in judgment. If you love them and you know they are gonna put their mouths or hands on you, distance yourself to protect them—not you! You are now the bearer of God's glory, and as such, you are holy!

Proverb of Fire 125
The people God has assigned to your life will receive you naturally. It won't be forced, manipulated or coerced. It'll

just happen, so stop trying to open your life to people whom God will ultimately have to deliver you from.

Proverb of Fire 126
Trying to buy love or friends is like trying to buy tickets to heaven. #AccessDenied

Proverb of Fire 127
Don't let the Lord find Satan's fingerprints on your heart or your bedpost.

Proverb of Fire 128
Unforgiving people run off memory.

Proverb of Fire 129
There is such a thing as being emotionally abusive towards yourself. This happens when you try to measure yourself by your works and not by your faith. Know this: The closer you get to God, the greater works you'll do. Don't beat yourself up about where you are today, otherwise, you will be your own abuser, and God will take you through a painful process of delivering you from yourself. Those of us who have been through this form of deliverance know how painful and lengthy it can be.

Proverb of Fire 130
You can't change God's mind. You have to let Him change yours.

Proverb of Fire 131
A cactus remains a cactus no matter where it's grown or where it's planted. It just grows better in some climates, but it does not change what it is when it's moved. Instead, it

changes its rate of growth. The same goes for a misled man. You can change his relationship status, location and his religion, but you can't change what he is.

Proverb of Fire 132
Anytime you approach God telling Him about the flaws in another person, He listens and then hands you a mirror.

Proverb of Fire 133
A pregnant woman expects a baby, just as a faithful servant expects a blessing.

Proverb of Fire 134
A blind man only sees darkness. Even when his eyes are open, his understanding is closed.

Proverb of Fire 135
Knowledge is natural; understanding is birthed when God opens our minds and gives us revelation of the natural. Wisdom is the knowledge of God supernaturally found in a natural man.

Proverb of Fire 136
Satan should not have you on his friend's list.

Proverb of Fire 137
Doubt is nothing but belief headed in the wrong direction.

Proverb of Fire 138
A person who wins the lottery isn't a winner. That person is a loser who has gotten an advance on his or her poverty.

Proverb of Fire 139
Before the Devil devours a man, he must paralyze him with doubt or fear.

Proverb of Fire 140
When a person doesn't like you, it's not always because of something you did. It's often because of that person's inability to relate to you.

Proverb of Fire 141
Grace is not a license to sin; it is the space to repent. God even extended grace to Jezebel, but she would not repent so she went from grace to the grave.

Proverb of Fire 142
A man who trusts his flesh is often humbled by his flesh.

Proverb of Fire 143
Daily confession is needed if you want to leave today behind when you step into tomorrow.

Proverb of Fire 144
Marrying an unsaved man and then dragging him to church is like jumping out of a plane without a parachute because you want to test the theory of gravity.

Proverb of Fire 145
Before you entertain the wrong man, remember this: You can't tame a snake. You can only charm it.

Proverb of Fire 146
When a man approaches you, he is looking to see how you identify yourself. This helps him to determine how he will

identify you, if he can identify with you, and whether he wants to get to know you better. If you don't know your identity in Christ, you will identify yourself as just another woman walking on the face of the earth. Because of this, you will draw men after your flesh and these men will identify you as your flesh. They'll want to groom your flesh, tear down your flesh, fornicate with your flesh, commit adultery with your flesh, feed your flesh—but they won't know how to identify with that eternal part of you that they need to identify with: your spirit. God hides a wife from her husband, and that man has to stay in Christ and pursue the will of God for his life in order for him to find his wife. When he finds her, God reveals to him those innermost parts of her that no man on earth could see. Because your husband gets to know the real you, he agrees with God's will for himself, and he decides that he wants to spend a lifetime with you. Once the two of you have confirmed your union through a godly marriage, it is then and only then that you can reveal your flesh to your husband. You can uncover yourself because he's covering you. You can submit yourself to him because he has submitted himself to Christ. Know this: The wrong man can touch you, but never reach you. He can identify you, but never truly see you. He can listen to you, but never truly hear you. He can please your body, but he'll disappoint your soul. Obedience is better than sacrifice.

Proverb of Fire 147
Never give in to people who've given up on you.

Proverb of Fire 148
Procrastination often breeds depression because our flesh wants to put things off, whereas, our spirit man desires

obedience. Anytime we procrastinate on something, we cause a divide within ourselves. This is why we hate thinking or talking about whatever we are putting off. Have you paid that bill yet? If not, notice the uneasy feeling that came over you just by thinking about it. You're uneasy because you are divided within yourself. Do what you need to do to get your peace back, and seek to keep your peace daily.

Proverb of Fire 149
God said to love your neighbor as you love yourself. The problem today is that many people don't love themselves, so their neighbors are in trouble.

Proverb of Fire 150
When you withhold your testimony out of fear, you deprive God of the glory.

Proverb of Fire 151
Strife starts where understanding ends. The problem with most people is that they don't want to be stretched to understand more; they want to minimize other people to fit into their understanding.

Proverb of Fire 152
Fornication clouds your judgment and locks you into a sound-proof soul tie.

Proverb of Fire 153
People often marry the potential of who their spouses can be, but divorce the reality of who they are.

Proverb of Fire 154
You can't always measure the character of a person by what

they have or have not done. A person's true character or danger often lies in what they have the potential to do.

Proverb of Fire 155
In the midst of all the wrongs that were done to you, God is still right. Don't lose your faith.

Proverb of Fire 156
Believe it or not, you defy the odds because of Christ Jesus.

Proverb of Fire 157
Love and lust cannot coexist. That's why people in lust-filled marriages don't get along when they're standing up.

Proverb of Fire 158
The music you listen to does affect your choices. Don't feed trash to your soul, otherwise, it will come out of your mouth, show up at your front door, kick you out of your blessings, and start getting mail at your address.

Proverb of Fire 159
If he tries to lead you into fornication, he is not the one. A man's leadership outside the marriage mirrors the way he'll lead while in the marriage.

Proverb of Fire 160
When the wrong man gets on one knee to propose to you, you may hear him ask, "Will you be my wife?" but what he's really saying is, "Will you be my future ex-wife?"

Proverb of Fire 161
Celebrities won't be celebrated in hell. Stop making idols out of people.

Proverb of Fire 162

If you're cursing like a sailor with the same mouth you quote scriptures with, your heart is a well organized landfill.

Proverb of Fire 163

Unity defeats the Devil; division invites defeat!

Proverb of Fire 164

Stop calling the Holy Spirit your gut instinct. Give Him the glory that's due to Him.

Proverb of Fire 165

A person who looks down on another human being is not worth looking up to.

Proverb of Fire 166

You can't divorce Satan if you've still got his stuff (mindsets, idols, associations, ungodly media, etc.) in your house. Some folks kick Satan out on Sunday mornings and let him come back on Sunday evening.

Proverb of Fire 167

God isn't a fact; He is the Truth. That's why science and atheists keep missing Him. They are looking for facts to prove His non-existence when He can only be reached by faith. That's why the Bible calls them blind. They are looking in the natural realm for a supernatural God.

Proverb of Fire 168

A woman pursuing a man is like a deer pursuing a lion. It's completely unnatural. Ladies: YOU...ARE...THE...PRIZE! Now go sit in the presence of God until you know just how valuable you are!

Proverb of Fire 169
Finding your way back into the perfect will of God is the same path that you'll need to take to find your way back to you. If you don't know who you are, it's because you haven't sought the kingdom of God and all His righteousness, and therefore, your identity has not been revealed to you.

Proverb of Fire 170
Pay attention to the direction of a man's leadership when you're courting him. If he leads or attempts to lead you into sin, he is NOT the appointed one!

Proverb of Fire 171
Hope is good, but faith is better.

Proverb of Fire 172
Have you ever noticed that anytime you say that you are a victim of someone's behavior, you have to identify the person who's victimized you? In other words, you give a faceless devil an identity. That's why forgiveness is necessary. People in unforgiveness make their enemies popular, but people who choose to forgive use their enemies as footstools. Because of this, they end up rising above them and standing at heights they've never imagined they'd venture into.

Proverb of Fire 173
The truth is—if you end up in a relationship with the wrong person and God suddenly gives you a new heart and a new mind, the wrong person won't be able to relate to you anymore. That's why you wait for the change to occur in you first so you can make the right choice the first time.

Proverb of Fire 174
Marrying the wrong person is a selfish thing to do. Think about it.

Proverb of Fire 175
Who can stop what the Lord has set in motion? Nobody!

Proverb of Fire 176
Satan's most effective weapon against you is you, but your obedience to God causes the enemy's attempts to overthrow you to backfire.

Proverb of Fire 177
Money isn't the only valuable seed; your time is also a seed. Be careful where you spend it because whatever you spend your time doing, you can expect an increase to come from it. So, if you spend your time gossiping, your words will increase against you, and not the person or people you are speaking against. If you spend your time complaining, your words will increase against you, and you will have whatever you said. If you spend your time praising the Lord, your words will increase for you, and God will give you many more reasons to praise Him. If you spend your time dancing, you'll become a better dancer; if you spend your time fighting, you'll become a better fighter, but if you spend your time laboring in the things of God, your increase will be the blessings of God. See your time for what it is: a seed. And spend it doing whatever it is that you want to see an increase of in your life.

Proverb of Fire 178
If God gave you the vision, He will give you the provision.

Proverb of Fire 179
People fornicate to get what's not theirs to begin with, but faithful people won't fornicate because they don't want anything or anyone that doesn't belong to them.

Proverb of Fire 180
The Devil is afraid of any believer who's not afraid of him.

Proverb of Fire 181
There is no concealer for an ugly heart.

Proverb of Fire 182
Love covers a multitude of sin, but lust uncovers a multitude of sinners!

Proverb of Fire 183
Some people are afraid of standing out. I'm afraid of fitting in.

Proverb of Fire 184
You should be honored to know that God wants to use you. Now humble yourself and let Him.

Proverb of Fire 185
Having a bad man who's a good provider is like having a gas stove that leaks. Sure, it may still work, but at some point, it's gonna blow up.

Proverb of Fire 186
David didn't confront Goliath with his own name because that would have meant he would have had to fight him in his own strength. He confronted Goliath in the name of YESHUA, which meant God had to fight him. Some of you keep getting

your butts kicked because you keep confronting your Goliaths in your own name.

Proverb of Fire 187
Loving God has to be intentional. You can't love what He can do for you more than you love Him.

Proverb of Fire 188
There are no happy endings in hell.

Proverb of Fire 189
Humility and humiliation are fraternal twins. Humility is when you acknowledge that you're nothing but dirt, but humiliation happens when your dirt is exposed.

Proverb of Fire 190
Some folks end up waiting 15 years for their God-appointed spouses because they court/ date people who are obviously not for them, and then, they ask the Lord to prove to them that the person they're seeing isn't the one. God has already proven Himself! He does not need to prove the person, especially when that person is living a life that God does not approve of! The key to the wait is listening to the heart of the person. Out of the abundance of the heart, the mouth speaks. If it barks, it's a dog; if it meows, it's a cat, and if it fornicates, it's a fornicator!

Proverb of Fire 191
Your body is the only system within this system that has its own government and members. Fornication is Satan's attempt to override the government of your body, and therefore, elect sin as the ruler of your members. When sin reigns, death rules. We are the temple of the Holy Spirit and

we have to present our bodies as living sacrifices, holy and acceptable to God so that we do not defile our temples and we do not allow the enemy to come in and wage war against our members. Fornication is only fun when it is not understood.

Proverb of Fire 192
How many tests do you have to fail before you realize that Jesus is the answer?

Proverb of Fire 193
Depression is the result of rejecting who you are to make others happy. Unspeakable joy is being who you are despite what others think of you. It's easy to find yourself by simply being yourself.

Proverb of Fire 194
A person who has phenomenal faith is offensive to traditional church-goers because, without knowing it, they walk about the earth as mirrors causing others to see their own reflections through them. People aren't mad at you; they are mad at their own reflection and that's why they keep trying to break you!

Proverb of Fire 195
When you write off "love" as a feeling, you have limited your understanding of love, but not its power in the natural realm. Love is supernatural, whereas, it cannot be seen, heard or felt, but it can be experienced. What we feel isn't love; it's our response to the presence of love. A mother loves her children, and we see the evidence of her love in the things she does and says, but we cannot see her love. Her

love for her children supersedes the natural realm and that's why should she lose a child to death, she anxiously waits to meet her child again in heaven. Her love didn't die with the child. Understand the supernatural power of love and you won't end up settling for a bunch of unsettled emotions masking themselves as love. Love is who God is, and that's why it never fails.

Proverb of Fire 196

Unforgiveness is a heart condition, not an attitude towards a particular person. That's why people who have ought in their hearts toward others are impatient, intolerant and cruel.

Proverb of Fire 197

What is a demon? It is a wicked spirit—a fallen angel. What is an unsaved man or woman? A wicked spirit, a fallen soul. Now do you understand why we have to be delivered from people just like we have to be delivered from demons?

Proverb of Fire 198

Your God-ordained husband has the right measure of faith to find you, the right amount of knowledge to understand you and the perfect measure of long-suffering to love you past your imperfections. Any other man won't do.

Proverb of Fire 199

Lukewarm saints are being preheated by hell. Be cool and repent.

Proverb of Fire 200

Fornication is submitting your body as a living sacrifice, unholy and unacceptable to God. It is to lay your body on sin's altar because you didn't believe the Word, but believed the enemy when he said a blessing would come out of your fornication. It is when you lay yourself down as an offering in your attempt to conjure up blessings.

Chapter 3

Proverb of Fire 201
Never see yourself through another person's eyes. Their vision of you is limited to their perceptions of you, but the revelation of who you are is given to you by the Holy Spirit who dwells within you.

Proverb of Fire 202
If you limit what you're willing to do for God, you limit the power of God in your life. You can pray down heaven, but you won't be able to touch it if you refuse to let God touch you.

Proverb of Fire 203
Love and faith are both supernatural. That's why the human mind can't comprehend them, even though your heart (your spirit man) can embrace them.

Proverb of Fire 204
Your character is made up of who you are consistently, not occasionally. It's who you habitually are, not who you aspire to be.

Proverb of Fire 205
If he's married, he is not your God-ordained husband. Stop pawning yourself away waiting on Satan's promises to come to pass!

Proverb of Fire 206
The tests come, but God has already given us the answers. If you fail the test, it's because you tried to take it yourself.

Proverb of Fire 207
Even though the truth is oftentimes the hardest pill to

swallow, it's the most effective one.

Proverb of Fire 208
You can't love God and hate His people. That's like telling a father that you love him, but hate his son. He won't be flattered.

Proverb of Fire 209
The spirit of rejection is so foul, ugly and vicious that it rips a person's self esteem to pieces, and even when that person gets saved, they have to undergo a process of being put back together again. After that, they have to battle the spirit of rejection constantly because it's a familiar spirit to them; it's what they know. For this reason, many in the church unfairly criticize, persecute and judge other believers because those believers don't open their hearts and lives to them easily. The truth is that people are cautious about who they allow in their lives and rightfully so! Nevertheless, someone who isn't fully delivered from the spirit of rejection or the mindset they acquired while being brutally attacked by that spirit sees another person's caution as blatant rejection, and they take offense. That's why we NEED to be fully set free; that way, when we attempt to enter another person's life, we won't be offended if they aren't reciprocal of us. The truth is —some folks (including myself) are so content with their lives that they don't just establish relationships with everyone who wants to have a relationship. If they did, they'd have to undergo being delivered from one person after the other until they finally learned how to do what Proverbs 4:23 tells us to do: Guard your heart! You'll know when you are fully free when you are content with the life God has given you and you're able to see another person's

walls for what they are: them guarding their gates!

Proverb of Fire 210
Ladies, don't belittle yourself. You should NEVER allow yourself to be some man's secret. If he can't acknowledge you in the light, it's because you're only valuable to him when the lights are off!

Proverb of Fire 211
Experience is a daredevil's way of getting the truth.

Proverb of Fire 212
You should never have sex with a man whose last name is different from yours unless, you're married to him and you just haven't changed it yet.

Proverb of Fire 213
People in unforgiveness are still fighting years after the fights have ended and their opponents have gone home.

Proverb of Fire 214
Your God-ordained husband is a part of your inheritance, but the wrong man is judgment manifested.

Proverb of Fire 215
Christians aren't supposed to purr at the Devil. We're supposed to roar at him.

Proverb of Fire 216
Some people truly do hate the Devil, but that does not stop them from serving him.

Proverb of Fire 217
There are no boyfriends or girlfriends in the Bible. Those are make-believe titles designed for folks who need titles before they give up the goods.

Proverb of Fire 218
A creation can't fix a creation; you need the Creator for that.

Proverb of Fire 219
Some folks abstain from holiness, chase prophecies and eventually find themselves seated in witchcraft establishments where familiar spirits tickle their ears and confuse their thinking. They end up having communion with fornicating prophets, reprobate apostles, and thieving pastors because they did not pursue God; they pursued miracles, signs and wonders. Get on your face, people of God, and ask the Lord to lead you where His Spirit is. If you don't, you just might be one of those folks who's breaking bread with devils and wondering why God is not showing up in their lives, finances, etc.

Proverb of Fire 220
Calling me the president of the United States does not give me the right to move into the White House. I would have to be elected and sworn in first! A man calling you his wife without making you his wife does not give him the right to lie with you. He needs to nominate you as his fiancé and then swear you in as his wife before you start performing the duties of a wife, otherwise, you're nothing more than a glorified bedroom buddy.

Proverb of Fire 221
A person whose vision of you is limited is a person whose

walk with you is limited.

Proverb of Fire 222
Never allow a man to make love to you while you're wearing your maiden name.

Proverb of Fire 223
Being anxious to marry will almost always lead you into sexual immorality. Be anxious for nothing! People who are impatiently pursuing marriage often erect themselves as idols, and then, get mad at God for not worshipping them.

Proverb of Fire 224
I sought to become an independent woman until the Lord brought me in His will, and made me dependent on Him.

Proverb of Fire 225
The Lord has placed you on a pedestal that only your God-ordained husband can reach. Don't lower yourself for anyone.

Proverb of Fire 226
Some people have passed you by because they could not see the anointing on your life. They went around you and celebrated others, not knowing that the very people they were celebrating had climaxed. They'd reached the peak of their success! But they did NOT know about you because God hid your identity from them. They looked straight at you but could not see the real you! But when your season of revelation comes, you will know them for what they are and not who they're pretending to be because you saw them without the mask! Once God reveals your identity, they will be humbled or humiliated!

Proverb of Fire 227
A little bit of faith can go much further than a whole lot of words.

Proverb of Fire 228
Love equals everlasting life; hatred equals everlasting torment. You choose.

Proverb of Fire 229
Satan gets people to turn against the God who loves them, and then, slowly poisons them through the very sin they've come to love.

Proverb of Fire 230
A man can never love you past his understanding of love.

Proverb of Fire 231
The truth won't stop being the truth just because you're rebelling against it.

Proverb of Fire 232
Women who marry the wrong men often find out this truth: You can tell the wrong guy everything there is to know about you and he still won't know you! That's because you can only loan your flesh to a man, but God has to give him the intimate knowledge of who you are within. God won't hand this type of wisdom to a man who doesn't know what to do with it.

Proverb of Fire 233
Some saints have poor night vision. They can shout when the lights are on, but when darkness comes around, they can't seem to find their way out of it.

Proverb of Fire 234
How poverty works. When money comes in, it's like having a mouse in your house— you won't rest until it's gone.

Proverb of Fire 235
Yesterday's lessons should be today's blessings. Even a blind man won't keep falling into the same holes.

Proverb of Fire 236
As long as you're a victim, you can't reap the blessings of an overcomer! That's why it's necessary for you to get out of your flesh and forgive folks immediately!

Proverb of Fire 237
Before you sow a seed, make sure the person you're sowing into is a garden and not a graveyard.

Proverb of Fire 238
Anything that thrills you outside of God's order is called perversion.

Proverb of Fire 239
Any woman can be found by a man, but a woman of God who trusts in the Lord will be found by the man of God appointed to be her husband. There are NO blessings in disobedience, neither can you find a crooked man and make him straight. Any man can mate with a woman, but it takes the anointed and appointed husband to unite with his anointed and appointed wife and birth children of covenant. And then he sticks around to raise them, provide for them and guide them. There are too many women out looking for a man, but a wise woman stays in the Lord and her husband comes looking for her.

Proverb of Fire 240
Beware of people who always show up when they need to harvest something, but are never around when it's time to sow. In the kingdom, you can't reap what you did not sow. Don't let them be in your garden reaping and thanking God for you, because the minute they think they have a harvest in their own fields, they'll close their field up to you, and they'll use the Bible to justify doing it.

Proverb of Fire 241
Experience may be the better teacher, but it's also the meanest teacher.

Proverb of Fire 242
You have to walk away from evil associations in order to grow in the Lord. Familiar people recognize you for who you were, not who you are and any change in you will be mislabeled. If you want growth, oftentimes you have to do the unthinkable: walk away from the familiar to walk into the unfamiliar land of blessings and favor.

Proverb of Fire 243
You can't choose *who* you want to be, but you can change around the letters of your life and change *how* you want to be.

Proverb of Fire 244
Name your price and Satan's ready to pay it for your soul! Some folks sell out for bicycles, while others sell out for luxury cars. Either way, they end up in the same place trying to peddle fire.

Proverb of Fire 245
Sexually impatient people fornicate, rush into marriage, and then over-sex each other until they find themselves needing something else to keep the relationship afloat. That's when they start courting and find out that they aren't compatible mates.

Proverb of Fire 246
Pay attention to math. If you put a minus sign (negative) behind anything, it takes away from it. Life works the same way. Whenever you are faced with a problem, you can complain (be negative), and in doing so, you take away the glory from God and cost yourself many blessings. Or, you can praise God (be positive), and in doing so, you give the glory to God and cause Him to add on to you. It's your choice what type of sign or wonder you want to be.

Proverb of Fire 247
Sleeping with an unsaved man, and then, taking him to church only confuses him and pushes him further away from God, instead of drawing him closer. You can't win a soul that you're sexing. Evangelism and fornication work don't play for the same team.

Proverb of Fire 248
Whatever challenges your life, in truth, is challenging your faith.

Proverb of Fire 249
Only flesh can minister to flesh. But, it takes a wise, Holy Spirit filled saint to minister to the spirit of a man.

Proverb of Fire 250

A misunderstanding is a missed understanding, meaning, you missed the opportunity to get understanding because you got in your flesh.

Proverb of Fire 251

Going through a trial? Plead not guilty. How can you lose when God is the Judge and Jesus is your witness?

Proverb of Fire 252

Depression is simply the presence of purpose coupled with the absence of action.

Proverb of Fire 253

Instead of always telling God what you want Him to do for you, try asking Him what He wants you to do for Him. In doing His will, you will find your answers, deliverance, resolution and peace.

Proverb of Fire 254

Marriage is like a plant. If God brought it together, He will maintain it. He will water it, nurture it, prune away anything that would stop it from growing and He'll plant it in a garden the enemy doesn't have access to. If you brought it together, you will have to maintain it and that's too much work. You will drown it with your tears, depend on it to nurture you, prune away at your guy until he's castrated or cut down and you'll root it in your insecurities, voids and needs. Don't build a God-instituted union on flesh. That's like building a million dollar mansion in a bad neighborhood and wondering why it keeps getting broken into.

Proverb of Fire 255
The right man will add to you (appreciate you), whereas the wrong man will subtract from you (depreciate you). Don't end up mentally bankrupt trying to hold on to a man who knows you physically, but does not know you by the spirit.

Proverb of Fire 256
If you've asked God to use you, get ready for Him to remove every hindrance in your life that's keeping Him from using you.

Proverb of Fire 257
When Satan attacks you, you're either "under attack" or the attacker is under your feet—defeated.

Proverb of Fire 258
When God rejects someone for your life, He's not saying that you're not good enough for that person; He is saying He has better in store for you! Stop trying to hold onto lessons! That's like crying because your report card says you've passed to the next grade.

Proverb of Fire 259
You can get with the wrong man, but you can't make him right.

Proverb of Fire 260
The Bible says that devils believe and they tremble. So, if they believe, does this make them Christian? No! They are anti-Christ, meaning, they are against Christ, even though they believe in Him! The same goes for many who call themselves Christians today. They believe, but they are against Christ and that's why they embrace sin, justify

sinners and question the people of God. Catch this: The anti-Christ spirit isn't always revealed through a person who does not acknowledge Christ as Lord; sometimes, it manifests itself in the self-confessed Christian who acknowledges the Word, but does not honor Him in his/her life.

Proverb of Fire 261
Pain makes you passionate. You'll passionately stay away from whatever and whomever made you feel it!

Proverb of Fire 262
You can't get what you want from God until you get what you need from God.

Proverb of Fire 263
You are your God-purposed husband's crown, but to any other man, you're nothing but a cap only fit to be worn in a certain season because you match his mindset. Any change in his life (good or bad) will mark the onset of a different reality, which will eventually translate to you no longer being a compliment or an accessory to his life.

Proverb of Fire 264
You cannot sign a cease-fire agreement with the enemy. Even though he may promise to stop attacking you, all you have to do is read the fine print and you will see where he tells you to go to hell.

Proverb of Fire 265
People who try to sex their way into a blessing always end up sexing their way out of one.

Proverb of Fire 266

One of the problems that many single women have is thinking that holding out from the wrong man will make him magically want to do right—this is not true. Abstinence does not guarantee you a good husband, but it can ensure that you do get married. But what woman wants to be married to an ambitious unbeliever who was so anxious to bed her that he decided to wed her? Obedience to God ensures that you will one day stand at the altar with Mr. God-ordained. Being abstinent with the wrong man will only cause him to act in desperation and marry you. Nevertheless, after the wedding, he's going to want to divorce your mind, but keep your body, and the only way this will happen is if you renounce your beliefs to follow his. To have an unbelieving man, you will first have to become double-minded and unstable in all your ways, because you'll end up sleeping with the Devil full-time, but visiting God whenever you get a free moment. Closed legs are only one part of obeying God. You still have to serve Him with your life, and wait on the promised one, otherwise, you'll end up with a very patient and ambitious devil.

Proverb of Fire 267

A man is raised, but a man of God is raised up.

Proverb of Fire 268

Holiness is the wedding gown that attracts your groom.

Proverb of Fire 269

Forgiveness is your spirit man's vehicle. You can't go anywhere if you don't have it.

Proverb of Fire 270

Sin doesn't establish love; it contends with it.

Proverb of Fire 271
If you've been praying and asking the Lord to deliver you from a situation or a person, your prayers may be in error. Sometimes, the wisest prayers are, "Lord, give me the wisdom I'm supposed to get from this situation or this connection, and keep me as I persevere." A pilot would be foolish to spend his time begging to get out of class, when what he needs to fly is within those classes.

Proverb of Fire 272
Satan uses people as bridges to cross over into the lives of people he ordinarily wouldn't have any access to. In other words, beware of, or better yet, be aware of your associations. Sleeping saints often wake up bound.

Proverb of Fire 273
Pray Away is the most effective devil repellent on the market today.

Proverb of Fire 274
When you open your Bible and try to understand the Word in the same manner in which you try to understand the words that come together to make a sentence, you'll miss understanding—or better yet, set yourself up for many misunderstandings. The Word of God is not written to be comprehended by man's intellect. You need the Holy Spirit for revelation.

Proverb of Fire 275
Success doesn't choose us; we simply choose to tap into the success that God has already placed on the inside of us.

Proverb of Fire 276
You can't shack with the Devil and expect the Lord to pay your rent.

Proverb of Fire 277
To seduce means to lead astray. If you use seduction to get a man, you're only allowing yourself to be devil bait designed to lead some man outside the will of God and into lust. Once he enters lust, he is on the devil's territory and your services are no longer needed.

Proverb of Fire 278
Everything that lives in the womb has a gestation period. If it comes out of the womb prematurely, it may not be able to survive on its own. In other words, stop trying to rush God. Anything He sends to us has to go through a process. Respect the process.

Proverb of Fire 279
Holiness makes demons flee because when they see someone walking in holiness, they don't see the person, they see God working through that person.

Proverb of Fire 280
I will never call another human being my everything or my rock. Those positions are taken.

Proverb of Fire 281
It doesn't matter what position you pray in if your heart is not in submission to God.

Proverb of Fire 282
The law of attraction says "like attracts like," meaning, we

attract only what we are. What's funny is that the Word says the same thing, so the "law of attraction" is just man's attempt to take credit for what God has already said. Pay attention to the men you attract to you. They speak volumes of you. Also, pay attention to who and what you're attracted to. If you find yourself attracted to an ungodly man, you need to head back to the altar for deliverance. A rebellious spirit is an ungodly spirit, and if you're attracted to ungodly men, it's likely because there's something ungodly going on in you.

Proverb of Fire 283
If a man says he doesn't want to ever get married or he doesn't want to marry again, don't waste your time trying to change his mind. Believe him and walk away.

Proverb of Fire 284
Sometimes, we get so caught up trying to force yesterday's seeds to produce a harvest that we fail to sow today.

Proverb of Fire 285
A religious saint is a person who is holy on Sundays, but they take the rest of the week off.

Proverb of Fire 286
You can't be who people want you to be and who God called you to be at the same time. Choose one.

Proverb of Fire 287
Sometimes, we can get caught up in the trends that the media says are beautiful and end up messing up the natural uniqueness of our Master's touch. Look in the mirror everyday and tell yourself the truth: you are beautiful!

Proverb of Fire 288
The number one cause for divorce is lack of knowledge. The sad part is that's fixable.

Proverb of Fire 289
Rage is murder in its teen years. Eventually, it will grow up, and you don't want to be anywhere near it when it does.

Proverb of Fire 290
Some women think that if they get their Ishmaels baptized, they'll magically turn into Isaacs. The truth is when you baptize a devil, it'll only come out of the water a wet devil ready to testify that it survived baptism.

Proverb of Fire 291
You can marry the wrong man, but you can't force God to accept Him.

Proverb of Fire 292
Being married to a religious devil is far worse than being married to a secular devil because the religious man doesn't know that he has a devil.

Proverb of Fire 293
Abstinence should NEVER be a tool used to "convince" God to send you your God-appointed husband; it is a sacrificial offering to God done out of love. When you try to move God with your works, you end up looking like Cain when God didn't accept his offering. Offerings are done out of love, not religious manipulation disguised as righteousness. Be pure, but do it because you love the Lord, not because you want something from Him.

Proverb of Fire 294
Church shoes and fancy wigs won't get you into heaven.

Proverb of Fire 295
A hell bound life is not one that's worth celebrating. Let the blind celebrate the darkness, but those who have eyes to see are to celebrate the light.

Proverb of Fire 296
A religious saint is an enemy of holiness.

Proverb of Fire 297
The "kind" of man you want isn't necessarily the "kind" of man you need. Anytime we have types, we are out of the will of God because we are doing what God told us not to do, and that is—leaning to our own understanding. That's why people with "types" often find themselves swinging from one relationship to the other with the same type of devil in a different man.

Proverb of Fire 298
The minute he tries to lead you into fornication is the minute you need to stop following him.

Proverb of Fire 299
Lust is candy-coated death wrapped in a label of lies.

Proverb of Fire 300
Either the man you end up with will be the son of God or he will be Satan, Jr. Let God choose for you. After all, He is all-knowing.

Chapter 4

Chapter 9

Proverb of Fire 301
People who are afraid of demons are themselves demon possessed or oppressed. The fear of God is the only perfect fear. Anything else is demonic.

Proverb of Fire 302
Life is nothing but a continuous shifting of comfort zones and new beginnings. Sometimes, we feel overwhelmed by what God is doing in our lives because our flesh likes the comforts of repetition, whereas, our spirit man needs to be challenged to grow. For example, a man who is perfect for you today might not be a good fit for you tomorrow because your mind is going to continue to change until you reach the fullness of who you are in Christ. That's why it's important to your life and success to seek first the kingdom of God and all His righteousness; that way, He can add everything else to you. You might be challenged today, but don't be intimidated by what you see or what you don't see. Just know that if you're not shifting, it could be because you're stuck. It's better to be moved by God than to be held back by fear.

Proverb of Fire 303
A woman who refuses to submit her mind to Christ will easily submit her body and soul to a man. Even though she goes to church, she has not yet realized that she is the church.

Proverb of Fire 304
Followers measure success by the opinions of the people they are following, but leaders measure success by the progress of the people they are leading.

Proverb of Fire 305
A womanizer has nothing but the women he's caught and

the lies he's used to catch them with. Never allow yourself to be on the wrong man's hook.

Proverb of Fire 306
Sometimes, God answers our questions with a question. That's because the answer is locked away on the inside of us, but we tend to hide it from ourselves with a little wall we so lovingly refer to as denial.

Proverb of Fire 307
To some guys, you are a good idea, but for the right guy, you are a God idea.

Proverb of Fire 308
Lust is the enemy of love—the two cannot and will not coexist. Lust can't turn into love, just as love cannot spring from lust. The two are just as much at enmity with one another as their fathers are at enmity with one another.

Proverb of Fire 309
We (human beings) make life a lot harder than it has to be because we repeatedly reject knowledge. We fight one another when we should be teaming up, we cry when we should be rejoicing, we complain about people when we should be praising the Lord, and we die when we could be living. Life isn't as hard as we make it out to be. When we embrace knowledge, we won't be so easily offended, hurt, or confused. We would spend less time thinking about what happened and more time making things happen.

Proverb of Fire 310
Some women want so badly to be called somebody's wife that they are willing to marry Satan.

Proverb of Fire 311
Faith without works is dead. Death without faith is hell.

Proverb of Fire 312
If he won't be faithful to God, he won't be faithful to you.

You can't sleep with a man, and then, accuse him of rape when he turns out to be the wrong man. You willingly gave yourself to him, which means, you deceived yourself before he was able to deceive you. The same goes with the enemy. You can't entertain the Devil, and then, accuse him of attacking you when he starts acting like the Devil. It's time to stop playing church and start learning to be the church!

Proverb of Fire 313
You are not pre-programmed to fall into the sins and traps of your parents or their parents. You are not programmed at all! You are made in God's image, therefore, you have a beautiful thing called will. What you will yourself to do will determine what you pass on to the next generation. Don't carry a generational curse to the next generation—let them inherit love, grace, understanding and prosperity from you. Break the curse!

Proverb of Fire 314
Your praise is only as genuine as your faith.

Proverb of Fire 315
Many of today's celebrities are nothing but the world's modern day versions of a golden calf.

Proverb of Fire 316
Never let your situation boss you around.

Proverb of Fire 317

I want you to close your eyes and imagine that it's sunny outside, and you're riding down the street on your bicycle. As you ride past a group of ladies, you overhear one of them saying that fried okra tastes better than boiled okra. You disagree, but you keep on peddling because you have a life. As you pass by a group of guys discussing their favorite basketball players, and no one even mentions your favorite player, but you keep on peddling because you understand that there are billions of people in this world and each one has his or her own opinion. You're not about to engage in some silly squabble with someone about who makes the best eyeshadow or who's the best preacher in your county; it's not that serious, so you keep on peddling. Now open your eyes and apply that same principle on social media. If someone's opinion doesn't affect your life, social status, social security check, paycheck, salvation or your good name, keep on scrolling. It's not that serious.

Proverb of Fire 318

Learn to be okay with being alone and that's when God will send you someone worth your time.

Proverb of Fire 319

The Devil should be hiding from you, not hiding with you.

Proverb of Fire 320

Sometimes, God will offend your reality just to open you up to the truth.

Proverb of Fire 321

The man you want and the man you need aren't always one and the same. Sometimes, the man you want represents the brokenness in you, and because he doesn't have the proper tools to fix a broken soul, he is "wanted" since he feels like a void-filler in that area. Nevertheless, in due time, he will only rip that hole even bigger because again, he is a human being, therefore, he does not have the tools to fix a broken soul. The man you need represents who you are and what you're called or appointed to do. He is on reserve for the whole you —the you that you took to God, submitted to God, and then, died to self so Christ could live through you. The man you need could stand right before you in your brokenness, and to you, he'd be invisible because he represents wholeness— something, in that moment, that you cannot relate to. That's why it is absolutely necessary for you to go before God and break before Him so that He can take the shattered pieces of your soul, remove the debris and the residue of sin from it, and make you whole again. It is then and only then that you'll be able to see, accept, love, and respect the man of God whom YAHWEH has assigned to your life.

Proverb of Fire 322
Love is the antidote for unforgiveness, but you must have understanding before you can get a prescription for it.

Proverb of Fire 323
Your comfort zone is your beautifully decorated prison cell. The amazing truth is—you have the key to free yourself.

Proverb of Fire 324
If he treats you like a Mrs. while you're still a Ms., he is calling you a whore. Sometimes, unspoken words sound off the loudest, but we refuse to hear the truth because it's offensive to the lies we've told ourselves.

Proverb of Fire 325

If you keep telling yourself that one of your rewards to your husband is sex, you are still fishing with dead bait. Understand that lust-filled sex is stimulated and appeased by the lies people tell themselves and the lies their lovers tell them. That's why when those same folks get married, the truth comes out, and they end up in sexless marriages. Nevertheless, the strength of a godly union is found in the truth. People who live transparently in Christ Jesus have great marriages and great sex because the Devil can't find too many doors to oppose their unions. In other words, their thoughts toward one another are godly, and not hindered by suspicions, questions or perceptions. But people who depend on their flesh end up with a shelf full of porn, a bottle full of blue pills and a bunch of man-made toys because they now have to "entice" or "bewitch" themselves before they can enjoy their spouses. Let God change your mind before you even ask for a spouse, otherwise, you'll run into marriage and throw your flesh around until the truth kicks you out of your own bedroom.

Proverb of Fire 326

Think about it. Culture and society teach us to place family and people over any and everything. What better way to drive a prophet from amongst his or her kin than to allow that prophet to grow up in the midst of people who share their blood, but not their God? Allowing the prophet to grow up in the midst of unrelated relatives is the fastest and most effective way to cause the prophet to not be bound by familiar obligations and expectations, but instead, cause the prophet to go on a journey to seek his or her own identity— that's when he or she has a tangible encounter with the

Lord.

Proverb of Fire 327
Selfish prayers don't invite blessings; they invite revelations wrapped in storm clouds designed to get you to humble yourself. If you refuse to humble yourself, the storm hits you hard enough and humbles you for you. This is so that you can cry out to God from a broken place— a place of surrender, rather than praying amiss.

Proverb of Fire 328
A lie is often popularized by the number of people who follow it. The truth is often discredited by the number of Christians who reject it.

Proverb of Fire 329
It is better to be your husband's crown than some man's trophy.

Proverb of Fire 330
When Satan sees the whole armor of God coming, he has no clue who's under it.

Proverb of Fire 331
If a man finds you before he finds Christ, you are going to find out why Christ wanted to get to him first.

Proverb of Fire 332
Maintaining your purity is basically you saying to every man who crosses your path, "Keep your hands off my husband's property." Faithfulness starts before you meet your husband, not after.

Proverb of Fire 333

When a legalist picks up the Bible, it isn't to learn the Word and better themselves. It's to learn how to address anyone who claims to know the Word; that way, they themselves can appear wise.

Proverb of Fire 334

Your marriage will only be as strong as your faith.

Proverb of Fire 335

Opportunities attract opportunists.

Proverb of Fire 336

Think about it— rejection by man is a form of flattery.

Proverb of Fire 337

Love never fails because God is Love. So, when someone says they love you, they are really saying they have God's heart for you. If they don't know God, they don't know love and this means that they don't love you; they are emotionally connected to you.

Proverb of Fire 338

When Satan throws a temper tantrum, just know that it's because you have something he wants, and he can't take it from you! His tantrum is his way of "persuading" you to hand over your blessings.

Proverb of Fire 339

You can't create a storm, and then, rebuke it. If you do, you first need to humble and correct yourself; it is then and only then that the storm will pass.

Proverb of Fire 340
Unforgiveness is a weapon pointed in the wrong direction.

Proverb of Fire 341
You are the answer to somebody's prayers.

Proverb of Fire 342
Beware of so-called friends who attack you without warning. Some people feel the need to attack their friends because they want to have something for the two of you to overcome together. Starting a fight is nothing but an instrument they use to finally tell you how they really feel about you. Once they've unloaded on you, they'll often come to you in what appears to be a humble, loving state saying that they value your friendship and hope that you don't end the friendship for a minor dispute. Please know that this is nothing but a passive-aggressive enemy—a sly serpent. That snake will get close to you and pretend to be non-venomous, but once it gets close enough to strike, it'll suddenly reveal its fangs and lash out at you. Oftentimes, you won't know how venomous it is until it's bitten you. When they see that the venom did not kill you or get you to turn away from your God-given assignment, they'll go back to pretending to be your friend, and they'll patiently wait for another opportunity to strike again. A snake is a snake—venomous or non-venomous! You cannot fellowship with it! Pay attention to the people around you. Sometimes, your breakthrough is being held back until you breakup with the people in your circle.

Proverb of Fire 343
People who are faithful to God often attract faithful spouses.

Proverb of Fire 344
Every day is an opportunity to sow the seeds that you want to reap the following day.

Proverb of Fire 345
If you want to know where God is trying to bless you, look for the area in your life that has the most opposition and then refuse to be moved out of your position by whatever's opposing it.

Proverb of Fire 346
Satan should never walk away from attacking you; he should either be running or limping.

Proverb of Fire 347
Know this: Demons are spiritually discerning too. They recognize their own. If you're demonically bound, sometimes the evidence is found in who's comfortable being around you, what people are comfortable doing around you, what people are comfortable saying to you and what people are comfortable doing to you. When you walk in holiness, you walk in authority and demons will avoid you like the plague.

Proverb of Fire 348
If you're not worth waiting for, he won't think you're worth fighting for either.

Proverb of Fire 349
Fornication is an orgy with the Devil.

Proverb of Fire 350
Know your worth or the Devil will discount you.

Proverb of Fire 351
Abstinence is a daily commitment; not a vow you take and then struggle with.

Proverb of Fire 352
Being called "sexy" isn't a compliment. It simply means the person who's referring to you by that term wants to have "sex" with you. In today's society, some men have found creative ways of calling women whores and some women are silly enough to be flattered. If he tries to pursue you as a wife without trying to have sex with you before you are his wife, it is then that he is complimenting you.

Proverb of Fire 353
Satan is scared that you'll find out that he's scared of you.

Proverb of Fire 354
The two greatest challenges we face in our walks are opposition and elevation. When we face opposition, our faith is being tested, and we'll either push ahead or turn back. When we're elevated, our humility is being tested, and we'll either become prideful and fall or humble ourselves and continue to stand on the Word.

Proverb of Fire 355
Many believers give sin free roam in their lives, all the while, attempting to put a leash on the Lord. That's why sin attacks them in whatever area they haven't submitted to the Lord. If you're tired of being attacked in your finances, submit your finances to the Lord. If you're tired of being attacked in your home, submit your household to the Lord. If you're tired of being attacked in your marriage, make sure you are submitted to the Lord, and He will deal with the spouse

through you. Give yourself wholly to God, and stop trying to give Him bits and pieces of you.

Proverb of Fire 356
Trying to open doors that the Lord has shut is as stupid as trying to high five a lightning bolt.

Proverb of Fire 357
You walk upright in the natural, and that's how God wants you to walk in the spirit. When the serpent deceived Eve, God cast the serpent on its belly because it had to walk in the manner in which it was. It was not upright, so it could not walk upright.

Proverb of Fire 358
People who rush into marriage simply because they are anxious to have sex often end up in sexless marriages. In the beginning, your top half can charge up your bottom half without any stimulation, but before long, your top half (mind) will need recharging. If your other half (spouse) can't stimulate your mind, your bottom half will need a boost....

Proverb of Fire 359
Wisdom is free, but it costs a lot to be a fool.

Proverb of Fire 360
Every time you open your horoscope, you open your heart to familiar spirits.

Proverb of Fire 361
Once you reach the limit of a person's understanding of you, you will enter into their perception of you. It is then that your season with that person ends because perception is

man's version of understanding, which is oftentimes a misunderstanding or missed-understanding.

Proverb of Fire 362
A religious man will defend his religion faster than he will defend God. Why is that? It's because his religion is his god.

Proverb of Fire 363
Kissing before marriage leads to lusting before marriage. What a lot of people don't understand is that you can enter a soul tie with a person from just a mere kiss. How so? Soul ties aren't always established through sex; soul ties are oftentimes established through association. Remember, David's soul knit with Jonathan's soul, meaning, they entered a soul tie with one another—and they were just friends! Every friend you have has a soul tie with you—believe it or not. The only difference is that your soul tie isn't established through sexual relations, nonetheless, it is a soul tie. Your belief system is established and runs from within your heart, so if you believe the person you're with is the one, you'll kiss the groom without hearing back from God. The soul tie was established through your relationship with that person and strengthened by a kiss. Now, the two of you are fighting off lust and trying to move the wedding date up because you've got your flesh involved in the relationship. Then, you end up married to the wrong person, trying to pray for God to enter a marriage when you kept Him out of the courtship. No. Remain pure. Remain holy. That way, you can see who the other person is without the blinders that are formed through soul ties.

Proverb of Fire 364
Holiness is the perfume of the meek, but religiousness is the stench of the proud at heart.

Proverb of Fire 365
Perception is a silent killer of the ignorant.

Proverb of Fire 366
An investment is giving of yourself to the point where you sometimes feel depleted. Spending is giving what you think you owe to get something in return. Don't invest the best of you in people who "spend time" with you.

Proverb of Fire 367
When a man reaches the end of his understanding, he starts to operate in his ignorance.

Proverb of Fire 368
A wise man is better than a wealthy fool.

Proverb of Fire 369
God will never be in an open relationship with you and the Devil. He has to be exclusive.

Proverb of Fire 370
Revelation knowledge is only for those who God desires to reveal Himself to, but don't despise who or what He chooses to reveal Himself through.

Proverb of Fire 371
The lessons of life are the blessings of life. It doesn't matter how wisdom has to find its way into your heart, if it gets in, you have been divinely favored by God.

Proverb of Fire 372
Satan is a liar! He doesn't "own" any blessings to give you!
He'll only teach you to tap into the blessings God has stored
up on the inside of you, and then one-by-one, turn every last
one of those blessings over to him. Remember, he is a thief
and a liar and the truth is not in him!

Proverb of Fire 373
A man who has not separated himself from the world is not
ready to be joined to a wife.

Proverb of Fire 374
In ministry, you will offend the double-minded when you
refuse to bend.

Proverb of Fire 375
A wife from God is a crown of glory to the husband who
wears her, but a foolish woman is a crown of thorns to the
man who wears her out.

Proverb of Fire 376
Most people don't get upset with the people who reveal
themselves as being temporary fixtures in their lives; they
get upset with themselves for thinking they were
permanent.

Proverb of Fire 377
If you can't stop thinking about what somebody said to you,
said about you or did to you, you are being stalked by the
spirit of unforgiveness. Bind it and move on.

Proverb of Fire 378
You can see a trial as a bad time or you can see it as an

opportunity. How you see the trial will determine what you get out of it.

Proverb of Fire 379
When you disobey God, it's because you are obeying your fears, and therefore, giving your fears the power to manifest themselves in your lives.

Proverb of Fire 380
Sex before marriage equates to you putting yourself before God. Anything that doesn't follow God's order is called disorder, and you can't expect it to serve as a blessing to you.

Proverb of Fire 381
Men show off their leadership skills during the courtship. If your guy is trying to lead you to the bedroom before changing your last name, he's pretty much telling you that his leadership cannot be trusted, and neither can he. If God can't trust him, why would you?

Proverb of Fire 382
Self-pity is a form of pride.

Proverb of Fire 383
You are a brand name, but it's up to you whether you end up being a generic copy of someone else or if you'll be the designer's label that God has created you to be.

Proverb of Fire 384
How ironic is it that people who find themselves burning with desire often end up getting burned when they act on those desires?

Proverb of Fire 385
Love has never lost a war and a true warrior never loses his or her love.

Proverb of Fire 386
Sure, we go through trials, but it is what you do with the knowledge you obtain in those trials that will determine whether those trials helped you or hindered you. At the same time, it is never wise to go through a trial and not ask God for the wisdom in that trial. Trials are like old caves. Sure, they may be dark and uninviting, but they almost always have something valuable in them.

Proverb of Fire 387
The tests of today are tomorrow's testimonies.

Proverb of Fire 388
Wisdom will invite you to her house, but she won't force her way into yours.

Proverb of Fire 389
The Bible tells husbands to love wives as they love themselves. The Bible also says that fornication is a sin against one's self! Listen up—If he's trying to fornicate with you, he obviously doesn't love himself, so don't get mad when he actually does love you in the same manner that he loves himself: null! Wait for the holy man, not the horny one.

Proverb of Fire 390
You can't give your time to Satan, and then run to God every time he starts giving you hell. In every relationship, there will be problems, and a person's relationship with Satan is no different.

Proverb of Fire 391
We're always secure when we know who we are, but we're insecure when we don't know who we want to be. Be yourself. You are an original.

Proverb of Fire 392
The one thing that's always under attack in your life is love. There are many people on the loose who don't have love in their hearts, and you're going to bump into them almost everyday. They will offend you, hurt your feelings, come after the people you love and they will come after the things you've worked hard to acquire. But in reality, the enemy's purpose for them is to get them to lure you into hatred, unforgiveness, strife, bitterness and wrath. He wants to get you outside of love, because outside of love, you have no covering. Outside of love, you can't be blessed. Outside of love, there is no protection for you. Outside of love, you will speak evil, receive evil and be evil. Whatever you do, don't let go of your love. Turn the evildoers over to God and He will return every blessing to you that's been stolen.

Proverb of Fire 393
Marrying the wrong man won't make him right.

Proverb of Fire 394
Righteousness is a flashlight that never goes off. That's why people in rebellion don't like when you're around.

Proverb of Fire 395
Faith is like medicine; fear is like poison.

Proverb of Fire 396
Don't mistake a smart man for a wise one.

Proverb of Fire 397
If he has no soul tie with you, he has no power over you.

Proverb of Fire 398
It is difficult for a man who does not respect women to get the attention of a woman who knows her worth; after all, how can two walk together except they agree?

Proverb of Fire 399
If he tries to take you to the bedroom without first taking you to the altar to marry you, he is silently calling you a whore.

Proverb of Fire 400
When you sin privately, God will allow the consequences of your sin to be broadcast publicly.

Chapter 5

Proverb of Fire 401
Jesus Christ has to be the head of your life at all times: When you're happy, when you're sad, when you're angry, when you're frustrated, when you're scared, when you're hurting and when you're elated. He can't just be Lord (Master) in the good times or the bad times. He has to be and remain the Lord of your life at all times.

Proverb of Fire 402
You can't call yourself a help meet if you don't know where your help comes from. A help meet must first help themselves, and then, they are able to aid their husbands. Don't rush towards marriage if you are coming in as a help meet who needs help.

Proverb of Fire 403
Your attitude has to be: There is no man cute enough, rich enough or powerful enough to make me sin against my God! If he needs a sin offering, he becomes a history lesson because he has made it clear that he is not to be a part of my future!

Proverb of Fire 404
Don't trust a leader who wears sheets on Sunday morning, but is between the sheets with someone who is not their spouse on Saturday night.

Proverb of Fire 405
Nobody in hell is horny.

Proverb of Fire 406
Sin is the only circus where the performers have to pay to perform.

Proverb of Fire 407

Just because he's in church doesn't mean that he's in Christ. Wait for the one who is the church and not the one who confuses the sanctuary with the church. Know this: People who confuse the sanctuary with the church are only holy on Sundays.

Proverb of Fire 408

Remember this: God wants your body too. Who you give it to determines the direction, purpose, and outcome of your sacrifice.

Proverb of Fire 409

Every day, you will be tested to see if you can handle the promotion that the next day has to offer.

Proverb of Fire 410

You were created by the Master, therefore, you are a Masterpiece.

Proverb of Fire 411

The right one has been praying for you, but the wrong one simply meets you and feels entitled to you. Never give yourself to a person who has not asked God for you in prayer.

Proverb of Fire 412

If you have to guard your purity against him, he is not the one. Some women actually do remain abstinent and get married to the wrong men because they didn't know the difference between a man who led them in purity versus a man they had to lead in purity. This sets the foundations for disorderly marriages, whereas, the wife takes the lead and the husband struggles to find his identity. This is the recipe for a Jezebel/ Ahab marriage. Know this: Abraham led his wife, but Ahab followed his.

Proverb of Fire 413
Satan's greatest deception was to convince you that you were worthless to God, but the truth is—you're so valuable that the enemy can't touch you. He can only mess with your head in hopes that you'll self-destruct. You are an invaluable, one of a kind treasure who God loves so much that He has awakened you to see another day.

Proverb of Fire 414
Every storm has an eye. If you trust God, He will be the eye who watches over you.

Proverb of Fire 415
People call celebrities their "idols" without even realizing what they're saying.

Proverb of Fire 416
People who don't invest in their visions are like people who don't put gas in their cars: they aren't going anywhere anytime soon.

Proverb of Fire 417
Marriages built on lust are as weak as the people who're in them. Marriages built on love are as strong as the God who established them.

Proverb of Fire 418
Love is not an emotion; love is a spirit. That's why love never fails. It is the heart of who God is. God is love and love never

fails because God cannot fail.

Proverb of Fire 419
The most foolish characters on earth read tons of books, and then, attempt to discredit the Bible based on what they read in those books. A believer, however, reads the Bible and discredits tons of books based on what he or she read in the Bible.

Proverb of Fire 420
You are a miraculous, supernatural manifestation that defies logic. That's why it's silly to stand behind science at the expense of your salvation.

Proverb of Fire 421
Sin is a foolish man's religion.

Proverb of Fire 422
God does not reward jealousy and there is no godly way to justify it. Jealousy is the evidence that you have submitted to a demonic spirit somewhere in your life because you've taken on the mindset of the Devil, as opposed to being thankful for what God has done for you.

Proverb of Fire 423
A husband is not a reward for your righteousness. He's just a dude on assignment.

Proverb of Fire 424
What God can't get you to hear (knowledge), He'll permit you to see (experience).

Proverb of Fire 425
Celebrate your victories while in the midst of your failures and you'll see brighter days!

Proverb of Fire 426
A witchcraft prayer isn't necessarily a prayer lifted up to devils by witches. A witchcraft prayer is any prayer that rises up against the will of God for your life, even when the person praying is attempting to pray to God. God says such prayers are amiss, meaning, they are inappropriate, and therefore, not received by Him. Nevertheless, just as they are released into the atmosphere, they should always be canceled out or returned to the sender. Right now, cancel all witchcraft prayers sent out against you in the name of Jesus, even those prayers you may have released. Today's a great day to change your reality, but to change what manifests as your reality, you have to change your mind.

Proverb of Fire 427
Fornication is the desecration of a holy place since you are the temple of the Holy Spirit.

Proverb of Fire 428
The reason it is a sin to call a believer a fool is because it undermines what Christ did for them on the cross. A fool is an unbeliever.

Proverb of Fire 429
There's never an excuse to be mad at or leery about anyone you have not prayed about unless you've seen their fruit!

Proverb of Fire 430
There is God's permissive will and there is God's perfect will.

What's the difference? God's permissive will is the place that you arrive at as the result of you making a choice that was not offensive to God, but it's not necessarily what He would have led you to had you sought Him. His perfect will is the place that you arrive at after you've sought Him, obeyed Him and followed Him thoroughly.

Proverb of Fire 431
If you think another woman or man is gonna cure you of that adulterous spirit, you've got another ex coming.

Proverb of Fire 432
Sometimes, the best way to fight back is to step back and analyze what's coming against you.

Proverb of Fire 433
Truthfully, we climb mountains and complain about them when we could've simply told them to move in Jesus name!

Proverb of Fire 434
Experience is a drunk man's sobering tool.

Proverb of Fire 435
Opposition is the opposing of your position. God opposes your position in sin and Satan opposes your position in righteousness. So, when you're in right-standing with God and someone opposes your position, that person is Satan-sent. When you're in sin and someone opposes your position, that person is God-sent.

Proverb of Fire 436
Rejection by man isn't always what it appears to be. Sometimes, man's rejection is God's way of forcing a person

to admit that they do not deserve you.

Proverb of Fire 437
You have to want God more than you want a man. You have to seek God more than you're seeking a man.

Proverb of Fire 438
There's nothing more demeaning than to have the world at your fingertips, but no power to reach it.

Proverb of Fire 439
Have you spoken to the weapons formed and declared to them that they shall not prosper? Have you spoken to the tongues rising against you and told them to hold their peace or be condemned by God? If you haven't, you're not fighting back. You're just fighting.

Proverb of Fire 440
What lies have joined together, the truth will put asunder.

Proverb of Fire 441
People who turn cartwheels can turn them because they have faith that they'll land on their feet once they've flipped. The greater their faith, the more creative and daring they are with their flips. People who can't turn cartwheels are fearful that they won't land on their feet, therefore, as they think in their hearts, they are! Fear stops people from doing amazing things. Pray fear away, and then, challenge it by doing what it said you cannot do!

Proverb of Fire 442
If it makes sense to the natural mind, it's not faith.

Proverb of Fire 443

A woman who walks around half naked is oftentimes curved in all the right places—except her mind.

Proverb of Fire 444

God isn't just looking for people to testify; He's looking for people who are willing to be living testimonies.

Proverb of Fire 445

It doesn't matter what your intentions are. God searches the heart of your motives, and if your motives are selfish and ungodly, you are working against Him.

Proverb of Fire 446

One of the smartest moves you'll ever make is to remove yourself from negative people.

Proverb of Fire 447

The power to get wealth is in YOUR creativity. Remember: God is the Creator, and we are His creations. Because of this, we are creative and our power to attract wealth is in our creativity. It sounds like a bad attempt at poetry, but it is the truth and anyone who embraces this truth will never be broke!

Proverb of Fire 448

Would you french kiss a snake? Anytime you lock lips with Ishmael, you are doing just that.

Proverb of Fire 449

Why are you asking God to bless your finances if you're bowing down to some illegal man in your bedroom?! Ask your idol to give you what you need.

Proverb of Fire 450
A woman who is married to another man (or multiple men) through fornication cannot be a man's favor until she is delivered (divorced) from her past lovers and her mind has been renewed. That's why many married men unknowingly marry married women and end up living under an attack. You can't take another man's wife and expect to be blessed. Ask Pharaoh. He begged Abraham to take his wife back.

Proverb of Fire 451
People often confess their fears and deny their faith. Remember, you shall have whatever you say.

Proverb of Fire 452
Before you judge what you do not understand, pray about it. Sometimes, people jump at the opportunity to speak before they've heard from heaven. Be quiet and pray first.

Proverb of Fire 453
You will always accept what you believe you deserve, even though you might not like it.

Proverb of Fire 454
It ain't faith until it offends religion.

Proverb of Fire 455
It's not about what God will do; it's about what He's already done. Religiousness speaks of God in future tense, but faith helps you to understand that He's always present and that it's already done.

Proverb of Fire 456
If he'll sin against heaven to have you, he'll sin against you.

Proverb of Fire 457
There is no deliverance where there is denial.

Proverb of Fire 458
Any ships you enter without God's permission are ships scheduled to sink, and they include: relationSHIPS, friendSHIPS and partnerSHIPs. If God's not onboard, it's gonna sink!

Proverb of Fire 459
Telling Satan to get his hands off you and canceling his attacks is not warfare; it's called exercising your legal rights through Christ Jesus. Binding the enemy that's attacking you, stripping it of its power and sending it to the abyss is minor warfare. Binding the enemy that's attacking you, the ones who have attacked you in the past, the ones who used other folks to attack you, the ones that have been attacking your loved ones, and the ones that have been attacking complete strangers, and then, using your legal rights to cast them into the abyss until the day of Judgment is the stuff that warfare is made of. The way to stop making yourself an attractive target for the enemy is by costing the enemy far more than what he's trying to take or has taken from you.

Proverb of Fire 460
You can change his relationship status, but you can't change his heart.

Proverb of Fire 461
If you're partly submitted to God, you're wholly submitted to the Devil.

Proverb of Fire 462
You can unscrew a light bulb, but you can't unscrew a man. Remember, sex is the one thing you can't take back.

Proverb of Fire 463
Humble, humility, and humiliation are all references to either reminding yourself that you're human or being reminded that you're human.

Proverb of Fire 464
Chasing knowledge while rejecting understanding is like filling up a gas can when you have no car.

Proverb of Fire 465
Heaven is the non-smoking section of eternity.

Proverb of Fire 466
Some women refuse to wait on God to send them the husbands He has chosen for them. Consequentially, they end up waiting two or three times as long for God to change the men who they chose for themselves. Single equals waiting in peace, not in tears.

Proverb of Fire 467
Be active, not reactive. An active person is set in purpose and is focused. A reactive person spends their life reacting to things said, done and heard, rather than focusing on their purpose. Be active, not reactive.

Proverb of Fire 468
The Devil lies to you so that man can lie with you. Illegal soul ties are the umbilical cords of hell.

Proverb of Fire 469
People in hell wish they could hear the word "repent" one more time.

Proverb of Fire 470
There are no couples in hell, just as there is no love in hell. Everyone in hell is single.

Proverb of Fire 471
Some situations don't bring out the worst in people, they bring out the truth in them.

Proverb of Fire 472
Disagreements are not indicators that you need to fight; sometimes, it's an indication that you need to shift physically, mentally or spiritually.

Proverb of Fire 473
Adultery is more than an act; it is a heart condition.

Proverb of Fire 474
Wisdom is a covering and if you let her cover you, you'll be like a crown covered in precious jewels and diamonds. The more wisdom you have, the more valuable you'll be. The more valuable you are, the greater the price the man has to pay to call you his wife. A man who can afford a wise woman is a wealthy many in the Spirit.

Proverb of Fire 475
A blessing is almost always mistaken for a curse when it's in the wrong hands.

Proverb of Fire 476
He has to love God enough to refrain from uncovering you before the wedding; that way, he'll love you enough to cover you after the wedding.

Proverb of Fire 477
Trying to catch a prophetic blessing while unrepentantly living in rebellion is like trying to catch a football at a basketball game.

Proverb of Fire 478
If everyone likes you, you may need to try speaking the truth more.

Proverb of Fire 479
Some people treat Jesus like He's past tense. Little do they know, He's always present.

Proverb of Fire 480
Sometimes a never-ending storm is God's way of flooding your comfort zone until you come running out of it.

Proverb of Fire 481
Beware of man-made traditions. They are bottomless pits that swallow up religious folks generation after generation.

Proverb of Fire 482
You look better being you than you do being someone you're not.

Proverb of Fire 483
Sin is a horrible boss. After all, it pays its workers with death.

Proverb of Fire 484

It is better to be single and waiting on God to send the man He's chosen for you than it is to be married and waiting on God to remove the one that you chose for yourself.

Proverb of Fire 485

What I've learned about leadership is that a leader picks up his or her cross to follow after the Lord. Jesus went to prepare a place for us, meaning, He went there first. A leader goes before the flock and is met by so many obstacles and wolves along the way. After overcoming devil-made traps and fleshly snares (through Christ Jesus), a leader must return to lead the sheep. That leader can help his or her followers to avoid certain roads because they've been down those roads and found them to be dead ends, traps, and roads to nowhere. Message: Never follow a leader who hasn't been through the fire. Anyone can preach a good sermon, but it's the fire of a trial that separates the faithful from the faint at heart.

Proverb of Fire 486

Disobeying God is a sin, even if it's done for a good cause.

Proverb of Fire 487

Pride is weakness masquerading as strength. Humility is strength disguised by meekness and is often mistaken for weakness.

Proverb of Fire 488

Going before the Lord and breaking on your own changes the status of a pending storm from necessary to unnecessary.

Proverb of Fire 489
Though they may look similar, orgasm and deliverance are not one in the same. You can't sex a devil out of a man. Many have gone before you and tried, but when the event was over, they were the ones who walked away needing deliverance.

Proverb of Fire 490
Do not be deceived. Your heart is the door of the church because you are the church! Be careful who and what you let in.

Proverb of Fire 491
We are all sheep being cared for by our Shepherd. With that being said, sometimes it's not the enemy attacking us. It's just that whenever we stray away from the Shepherd, trials and tribulations become the sheepdogs that herd us and drive us back into our Shepherd's will.

Proverb of Fire 492
God is in the blessing business; Satan is in the stealing business. Be careful that you don't open the door for the thief and expect a blessing to come in.

Proverb of Fire 493
Faith and common sense are mortal enemies because faith will have you doing things that common sense says you should not do and believing God for things that common sense says you can not have.

Proverb of Fire 494
God is present tense. Anything that reads as past tense in the Bible is already done, meaning, you're already healed,

delivered, set free, and saved the minute you believe God for it. That's why it's error for you to WAIT for God to answer your prayers; they're already answered. The only thing you're waiting on is the manifestation of what you've been praying for OR the revelation that your prayer was amiss because your motives were impure.

Proverb of Fire 495
Closed doors don't make sounds. In other words, the noise in your life is coming from the doors God has commanded you to close that you're struggling to keep open.

Proverb of Fire 496
Asking God for permission to marry the wrong man is like going to Burger King and asking for a Big Mac.

Proverb of Fire 497
Satan has some folks on his hit list while he has others in his little black book.

Proverb of Fire 498
Satan goes into church buildings and he will hoop, holler, and hiss wherever there is religion, but no Holy Spirit. How do you know what churches are God-filled versus the ones that are full of religious devils? The Bible says you will know them by their fruit. Look at the members! If the head is sick, so is the body. If you don't see the fruit of the Holy Spirit, don't you dare touch the doors of that building unless God says otherwise.

Proverb of Fire 499
Forgiveness is more important than your next breath.

Proverb of Fire 500

What he said: "I'm not a spiritual person. No, I don't read the Bible. No, I don't go to church, but I believe in God. Maybe you can teach me more about God." What I heard: "The Jezebel spirit is hiring spiritual pedophiles who are too desperate to wait. Would you like to apply?"

Chapter 6

Chapter 6

Proverb of Fire 501
Time doesn't heal wounds; it only teaches you to live with them. God heals the brokenhearted.

Proverb of Fire 502
Who you are and who people want you to be can never coexist. Be who God designed you to be. That's where your peace is.

Proverb of Fire 503
To make a mistake; that's normal. To not learn from that mistake, now that's a problem.

Proverb of Fire 504
Opposition is the demonic opposing of your God-appointed position!

Proverb of Fire 505
The Word is the only power that can never black out.

Proverb of Fire 506
Satan's hit song, "God Knows My Heart" is still number one on the charts of religiousness.

Proverb of Fire 507
There is a difference between sowing and burying. Know the difference or you'll bury your seeds and wonder why they aren't producing a harvest.

Proverb of Fire 508
A man can want to have kids with you, but have absolutely no desire to marry you. For him, giving you kids is no different than marking his territory. If you ever walk away

from him, he will walk away from his kids.

Proverb of Fire 509

Your capacity to love represents your capacity to be blessed. That's why most folks with limited love live limited lives.

Proverb of Fire 510

Some people love the prophets of God until they realize that true prophets have to tell the whole truth and not just the truth they like.

Proverb of Fire 511

I looked to the left and I saw my reflection. She was weeping. I looked to the right and I saw my shadow. She was running, but there was nowhere for her to go. I looked beneath me and I saw a bottomless pit—there was no hope. I looked up and I saw the life I'd rejected. I didn't see heaven when I looked up. I saw normal, happy people enjoying their lives. I had chosen the pit I was in. I'd fornicated my way into two marriages and just when I went to collect my prize, there was nothingness—barrenness—despair. I cried out to God the first time and after what felt like forever, He delivered me, but I had not yet fully learned my lesson, so I made my way to the altar through the bedroom once again. Again, I went to every corner of my life looking to collect my reward, but there was nothing but emptiness. Finally, I cried out to God and I repented—truly repented for my choices. I told the Lord that if He delivered me, I would never fornicate again, and for a long time, it was as if God did not hear me.

He left me in that dark marriage and He only gave me enough light to find my way back to Him. I wanted to get out of the dungeon I'd gotten myself into, but God wanted me to get to know Him. It took me being in that dungeon to finally submit myself wholly to Him—no more religious games. The light that led me to Him also led me to freedom. Before I left that pit, I chose to give God another promise—one that would challenge the very fabric of my faith: I promised God I would not kiss a man; I would only kiss the husband He has appointed for me when we got to the altar and got permission from the pastor to kiss one another. I teach against fornication with fire because it was the tool the enemy used to ensnare me, so I won't shut up about it, and I won't be intimidated. I am against fornication in every form because fornication is against me and it is against the One I love: YAHWEH!

Proverb of Fire 512
People who spend their time trying to get folks to like them often overlook the people who love them. God never commanded anyone to like anyone, so if you're trying to win man's favor, you are chasing the wind. God commanded us to love one another and if a person doesn't have the capacity to love you, you shouldn't care whether they like you anyway. Love and be loved; embrace the ones who love you and pray for (not against) the ones who don't. You have the power to change how you feel about not being liked; it's your choice.

Proverb of Fire 513
Get so far into holiness that the only man who can reach you is a man who lives there.

Proverb of Fire 514
If you ever want to find out how someone truly feels about

you, disagree with them.

Proverb of Fire 515
Bondage affects your spiritual sight, so if you're having trouble seeing what you've been praying for, stop looking for the blessing and start looking for the cords that are binding you. Denounce them, sever them, repent of them and tell them that they cannot reconnect—ever. After that, look again.

Proverb of Fire 516
You can't be delivered from what you keep delivering yourself to! If you want to be free, act like it.

Proverb of Fire 517
Hope and faith are not one in the same. Sometimes, we have trouble receiving the answers to our prayers simply because we didn't have the faith to receive what we've been praying for. When we don't have faith, we tend to put a mask on hope and try to pass it off as faith, hoping that God won't know the difference.

Proverb of Fire 518
Darkness is not a shortcut to the light.

Proverb of Fire 519
Where are your blessings? Locked up in a vault called truth, and the key to that vault is called faith. Even after you unlock it, you need the strength to open that vault. Your strength is called obedience, but your weakness is your disobedience.

Proverb of Fire 520
It is better to look for what you're doing wrong, rather than

what you're doing right. That way, you can advance towards improvement rather than being somewhere boasting and stuck with no advancement.

Proverb of Fire 521
If you want folks to like you, you are not ready for ministry. Ministers step on toes that they didn't even know were in their paths.

Proverb of Fire 522
The strength of the Devil in your life is equivalent to the amount of time you allow him to entertain your imaginations.

Proverb of Fire 523
If you tell peace to be still, yet, you keep moving, you didn't lose your peace—your peace lost you!

Proverb of Fire 524
Life isn't about continuing in another man's legacy; it's about starting your own.

Proverb of Fire 525
A woman who waits on the Lord is a wife worth waiting for. A man who submits to the Lord is a husband worth submitting to. Everyone else is just a counterfeit.

Proverb of Fire 526
A gossip's greatest fear is being gossiped about.

Proverb of Fire 527
Be sure to love people, but if you've literally got to love the hell out of them, you need to do so from a distance to

ensure you don't get burned.

Proverb of Fire 528

Life is easier when taken in small doses. One day at a time with one prayer at a time.

Proverb of Fire 529

No matter what happens in your life, be thankful to God for your life. What we often see as bad is really a set up for the good.

Proverb of Fire 530

Some men will come along and want you in the wrong way, but if you're not careful, you'll get caught up in the fact that they want you.

Proverb of Fire 531

If you tell a man that you're practicing purity and he doesn't call you back, stop calling him! If Satan is trying to flee from you, why would you chase him down?

Proverb of Fire 532

There is greatness in you. Tap into it by faith or let the seasons come upon you and find you like that barren fig tree, having borne no fruit. Remember, the tree that bore no fruit did not receive a blessing from Jesus. It was cursed.

Proverb of Fire 533

If God can make your heart beat without your help, He can change your situation without your help.

Proverb of Fire 534

At any given moment, we are pregnant with a blessing or a

consequence. Make sure the seeds you are sowing today are the harvest you'll want to give birth to tomorrow.

Proverb of Fire 535
A servant is never greater than his master, so if sin is your master, you couldn't be any lower.

Proverb of Fire 536
If God said yes to us every time we asked Him for something (or someone), we'd be dead, crazy, homeless or suicidal. When God says no, it's because what you're asking for is not a part of His plan for you. He says no to protect you. So, rather than questioning Him, why not just thank Him for every no He has ever said?

Proverb of Fire 537
When you're married, your spouse expects to not only have intimacy with you, but they want passionate intimacy. The difference between intimacy and passionate intimacy is intimacy is an expression of love, but passionate intimacy is an expression of love and appreciation. You can appreciate someone and not love them, but you will not love what you do not appreciate. To appreciate doesn't necessarily mean to be thankful for; to appreciate simply means to recognize the full worth of something. Do you appreciate God, meaning, do you recognize His worth? If you do, you won't just worship Him, but you will passionately serve Him. Your worship to God is your intimacy with Him, but it is your obedience to Him that serves as your passionate intimacy with Him. God doesn't just want your worship; He wants your obedience.

Proverb of Fire 538
Love never fails, but people do.

Proverb of Fire 539
If you publicly promote your sin, sin will publicly bring you down. Everything that starts in front of an audience, ends in front of an audience.

Proverb of Fire 540
The worst thing you could do to someone who hates you is to love them in return.

Proverb of Fire 541
When wisdom is above your understanding, you don't puff up against it; you humble yourself so you can receive it.

Proverb of Fire 542
The hardest tests in life that we have to take are the ones created by people because the answers are opinion-based and not truth-based. The easiest tests in life are the ones we face in our day-to-day lives. With man's tests, each problem has a different answer, but with the tests of life, the Word of God is always the answer. The Word encompasses love, faith, patience, knowledge, perseverance, and understanding. With the Word, you can never fail the test, but anytime you tap into the flesh for answers, you will fail miserably and that's a test you may have to retake!

Proverb of Fire 543
Believe it or not, when you got saved, you became a part of the supernatural.

Proverb of Fire 544
Not everyone who celebrates you publicly is celebrating you privately.

Proverb of Fire 545
Fornication is a weapon that Satan encourages people to use against themselves.

Proverb of Fire 546
A wise servant listens to even wiser servants; a foolish servant has to be taught by experience.

Proverb of Fire 547
Persecution is a dull sword until it's yielded by someone you respect. Esteem no one! Love your brethren, and give honor to whom honor is due, but never esteem one person over the other, otherwise, you will hand Satan a sharp weapon to throw at you.

Proverb of Fire 548
There are people out there who want to see you fail. Please disappoint them.

Proverb of Fire 549
There's an ocean of wisdom in every storm.

Proverb of Fire 550
Woman of God, you are so invaluable that there are countless men who'd like to sample you, but if you allow them to do so, you would devalue yourself. This would make it easier for the destroyer to send the one he wants to use to destroy you, your name, your character or your sound mind. But if you dare to know your value outside of what you see

in the mirror, you'd humbly wait for the one who can spiritually afford to take you off the market permanently. Stop letting folks sample you. You're better than that!

Proverb of Fire 551
Don't confuse head popping, eye rolling, attitude-filled religious statuses with an uncompromising Word of Truth. Oftentimes, what you are witnessing is an angel of darkness masquerading as an angel of light, but try as it may, it can't hide its bitterness.

Proverb of Fire 552
A manipulative tongue is one that has a fork in it.

Proverb of Fire 553
When you submit your mind to lies, you will submit your body to a liar. Guard your heart.

Proverb of Fire 554
Any man who offers to have sex with you outside of the covenant of marriage is not offering to love you; he is threatening to uncover you and expose you to the enemy for his own selfish gratification. Don't get flattered when you should be offended.

Proverb of Fire 555
Where love stands, Satan must bow or flee.

Proverb of Fire 556
Love covers a multitude of sins, but it does not justify them. Christ justified the sinner, not the sin.

Proverb of Fire 557
Don't bury what's alive and don't exhume what is dead!

Proverb of Fire 558
You can't choose a team, and then, fight your teammates. If you do, you need to sit on the bench until you are old enough to play with the big girls.

Proverb of Fire 559
Yesterday is the past. If you've let the sun set on your wrath, and carried an issue into today, you are no longer just angry; you are in unforgiveness. Let it go.

Proverb of Fire 560
The closest proximity to God is oftentimes the furthest distance from ourselves.

Proverb of Fire 561
We go from glory to glory and a woman of God is supposed to go from safety to safety. She leaves the safety of her father's house to enter the safety of her husband's arms. If her natural father is not in her life, God will provide her with a secondary father in the form of her pastor. When her husband finds her, he must first speak to her protector after he's spoken with her Almighty Protector. Before God and man, he must commit to loving, protecting, providing for and covering her all the days of his or her life. After he has received her at the altar from her protector's hands, made his vows to her in the presence of two or three witnesses and has been declared her husband, he may then kiss the bride. It is then that he has permission to uncover her body because he has vowed to cover her soul! If this order is violated, disorder is sure to follow! Woman of God, go from

glory to glory and protection to protection. Don't let some man convince you to meet him at the sacrificial altar that is his or your bedroom before he has paid the price for you! Only thieves steal brides.

Proverb of Fire 562
A made up mind is your life's turn signal. It signals a certain change. A double mind (uncertainty) is the poison that intoxicates the faithless and causes them to be all over the place. It signals an impending collision. Make up your mind and keep your mind stayed on Christ And you will arrive at the destination God has called you to.

Proverb of Fire 563
Don't make permanent decisions while in temporary mindsets.

Proverb of Fire 564
Religion will deafen a blind man, but holiness is the light that leads to everlasting life.

Proverb of Fire 565
A pregnant woman not only knows that she's going to give birth to a child, she also knows that she's going to go into labor if she is delivering the child naturally. This means that she will try to physically, mentally and spiritually prepare herself for the pain ahead. Listen up: We won't always have great days, but we are assured that there are some storms ahead. These storms precede some of our greatest blessings, so it's wise to not just focus on the blessings, but prepare yourself for the storms. Many blessings were terminated in the delivery room because the birther anticipated the

blessing but forgot to prepare for the labor.

Proverb of Fire 566
Woman of God, wait for the man who wants to cover you, not the one who wants to control you.

Proverb of Fire 567
Life is a vault full of treasures that only faith can unlock.

Proverb of Fire 568
The season of pruning is one of the most important seasons that there is! It is NECESSARY for a godly harvest. The problem with so many people is that they don't know how to identify seasons. Every season produces something and every season requires something. If you don't know how to recognize what season you're in, you're going to find yourself sowing when you should be reaping, and reaping when you should be sowing. You'll also spend pruning season arguing with the folks who God wants to prune from your life! You'll keep trying to teach them how to treat you and what is and is not acceptable behavior. Consequentially, those people will be the very tools Satan uses to choke the life out of the seeds you've sown! Before long, you'll become a religious sower, sowing nothing but mere words, chanting over other folks seeds and grabbing at every prophetic message you see that's released over God's people. Don't be that person whose faith dies because they had the faith, but no works and they couldn't pull up a harvest that they had not sown! Take God at His Word and learn to identify the seasons. Sow good and not evil, water your garden with praise and learn to prune away folks when their thorns start pricking you and choking the life out of your praise!

Proverb of Fire 569
Why would you fear the names of men when the Name above all names has authority over them?

Proverb of Fire 570
Embrace your uniqueness. It is what sets you apart.

Proverb of Fire 571
A foolish person's most fertile years is oftentimes the years when he or she has the least sense.

Proverb of Fire 572
When we stand before the living God, we won't be wearing wigs, weaves, makeup, perfume or contact lenses. We will come before Him as we are—no filters. That's why it's important to perfume your heart with knowledge, adorn your thoughts with understanding and to walk in the beauty of holiness. When we approach Him, we don't want to be an abomination and a reproach to Him; we want Him to see Christ in us so that we will attract His favor, blessings, and His everlasting presence.

Proverb of Fire 573
Arguing with a fool is the same as agreeing with him.

Proverb of Fire 574
The Devil doesn't mind you hoopin' and hollerin' in church when he knows he has you hoopin' and hollerin' in fornication. Choose ye this day whom you will serve.

Proverb of Fire 575
Ladies, there's a difference between religious control and submission. Submission is what we do freely because of our

love and fear of God, but religious control is women in bondage who do what they're told because they fear the people who head up that religion or because of lack of knowledge. A woman who doesn't have an intimate relationship with God will not know how to submit, so she may find herself a slave of religious control and manipulation. A woman who fears and loves the Lord will submit of her own free will because God has given her an understanding of what it means to submit. Because of this, she'll know the value of submitting to her husband and she'll demonstrate her knowledge of the Word through her submission. In this hour, God is calling us (both men and women) back to Him, to an intimate relationship with Him so that we can hear and recognize His voice for ourselves; that way, we don't keep falling into the pits of blind men and women.

Proverb of Fire 576
Understand this: Somebody is using you. You can either let God use you or you can allow the enemy to use you—either way, you're gonna be used by someone.

Proverb of Fire 577
Just when it looks like God has lost because of His silence, a mighty roar comes out from the other side of the hill and the enemy realizes that your help has come. Satan NEVER wins!

Proverb of Fire 578
If you measure a man by his height, you'll never be able to reach him.

Proverb of Fire 579
Woman of God, you don't have to be seductive to attract your God-ordained husband. As a matter of fact, seduction will repel him because it's designed to appeal to the flesh, whereas, your God-ordained husband will be searching for you in the realm of the spirit. Flesh attracts flesh and flesh attracts devils. A holy woman is so supernaturally unique that flesh-led men will repeatedly pass her by, but a man who's led by the Spirit of God will notice the God in her first. Don't let Hollywood teach you how to attract a devil to yourself; let the Word teach you how to be just like God: holy. That's when the unholy things will pass you by and you can truly say that you are ready for your God-purposed husband.

Proverb of Fire 580
Sin is the only authority that will read its rights to you before binding you. Stay free, my friend.

Proverb of Fire 581
Be careful that you don't attempt to curse God's people simply because they've offended you. Understand that when God said to touch not His anointed, He wasn't talking to the world, He was talking to the church! In other words, being a Christian doesn't give you the right to curse other Christians.

Proverb of Fire 582
Grace is not an excuse to sin. Grace is an extension of God's love, and if you love Him back, you won't take grace for granted.

Proverb of Fire 583
The flesh has the belly of hell. It cannot be quenched; it can

only be momentarily appeased.

Proverb of Fire 584
Wisdom is as different from intelligence as the sun is from a flashlight.

Proverb of Fire 585
It's time to stop ignoring what's right before our eyes and start making the necessary adjustments.

Proverb of Fire 586
One woman has been abstinent for 12 years and is still waiting for her God-appointed husband. Another woman has been abstinent for one year, and she has been found by her Mr. God-ordained. God doesn't move by seniority, nor are we able to take a number and have a seat in religiousness. Instead, God moves in our lives when our minds change. The lady who's been waiting 12 years has likely been entertaining the same mindset, devils, and people for the last 12 years, whereas, the woman who waited one year made the necessary sacrifices to please God. He then determined that she was "ministry-ready" and since marriage is a ministry, He revealed her location to her God-appointed husband. If you don't change your mind, God won't change your status.

Proverb of Fire 587
God is not asking you to make a sacrifice; He is requiring that you be the sacrifice.

Proverb of Fire 588
The Devil's favorite meal is sin-smothered saints with a side of religiousness, but righteousness is poisonous to him.

Proverb of Fire 589

A poor man with love has more to give than a rich man who has no love.

Proverb of Fire 590

There are people who aspire to do great things, and then, there are people who step out and do great things. One thing you need to know is that if you have a call on your life to move mountains and shift atmospheres, you are going to endure some persecution and the level of persecution you endure is a reflection of the level of the anointing on your life. That persecution is going to come at you in ripples, but it will never be more than you can bear and it doesn't start off as blatant persecution. In the beginning, it starts off as subtle persecution, whereas, some of the people who've managed to get close to you OR close enough to you will ever-so-nicely tell you their opinions about you, what you're doing and what they think you should be doing. This is subtle persecution. This is the way the enemy presented himself to Eve. He spoke lies to her in a friendly tone. He intentionally deceived her. Guess what? He does this same thing today, only through people. With subtle persecution, a person will smile at you while pointing you in the wrong direction. They'll even give you a hug before sending you off towards your own destruction. You won't know who they are until you REFUSE to do what they say. When you ever-so-lovingly match their smiles and kind tones, all the while, giving them a "no" that they did not expect, that's when they'll show their fangs. Learn God's voice and don't move until God says move. That way, when the smiles go away and the fangs come out, they won't be fighting up against a disobedient soul who's gone outside the will of God, but they'll be striking towards an obedient, God-fearing soul, and by doing so, they'll rise up against God, Himself. That's a fight that's already won.

Proverb of Fire 591
A religious man's religion is his god, but to a holy man, God is his religion.

Proverb of Fire 592
Love is eternal, and it doesn't matter how the seasons change, love will always remain. But unlike the things of the natural, love grows, but it cannot die. Love is selfless and love gains its momentum when it is truly embraced. Love can be warm, but it cannot be cold because it lives and comforts, but it is not a burden. Love carries its own weight, but the selfish burdens of man are too heavy to be carried.
Nevertheless, many do not know love; they know the emotional aspects of what they think love is, but they do not know true love because when the seasons change, what they have does not remain. It withers and dies because it was not love; it was the enemy of love: selfish ambition.
Nevertheless, the seasons will come and try everything that calls itself love, and the seasons will come and try everyone who says they love you, but if what they have for you is not love, it will not make it past the trying seasons. It'll puff up, and then, fade away because, just like false prophets and false teachers, there is a false love that is common amongst mankind, but when it's tried with fire, it's consumed. When true love is tried with fire, it only grows up and consumes the fire that's trying it.

Proverb of Fire 593
Why should you wait on God for your husband? Consider this: At this VERY moment, some woman out there is saying "I do" to the man who's going to eventually take her life.

Proverb of Fire 594
If your relatives are related to Satan, they are no longer your relatives if you belong to Christ. The blood of Jesus redeemed you from your family's bloodline.

Proverb of Fire 595
A woman who tries to change a man has a god complex. It won't be long before she realizes that she is not God.

Proverb of Fire 596
Everybody alive has sown something, but we won't always know what a person has sown until the reaping season.

Proverb of Fire 597
Stop scratching the surfaces of issues and start dealing with the root itself.

Proverb of Fire 598
There are too many twos (couples) becoming one without the presence of the third fold, Jesus Christ.

Proverb of Fire 599
The Devil is not "attacking" you if you serve him. He is devouring you. The difference is as obvious as a chicken fighting another chicken versus the chicken at KFC.

Proverb of Fire 600
Your perception of someone will determine how you treat

them and vice versa. Perception stems from ignorance, in most cases. How so? It is the result of entertaining a series of thoughts about an individual OR allowing someone else to sow a negative seed in your heart about that person. If perception isn't dealt with, it becomes full blown ignorance, or better yet, a belief system. When a thought is just a perception, it hasn't been believed yet, meaning, it has not settled itself in that person's heart, but once it becomes a belief, it becomes a heart condition. Thoughts that are contrary to the truth have to be cast down, but beliefs have to be cast out. Once your perceptions become beliefs, they set the stage for unforgiveness, hatred, strife, dissensions, witchcraft, envy, discord and every other vile manner of the flesh. In other words, perceptions and discernment are not one in the same! Discernment is spiritual, whereas, perception is fleshly rooted. For this reason, if someone tells you their perception of you, your response should be, "Your perception is your deception, not mine." Be careful that you don't allow negative thoughts to form in your mind about the people you are connected to. Confront your thoughts, ask questions and be more determined to move forward in love than you are to stay behind entertaining a bunch of deceptive thoughts designed by the enemy to lead you astray.

Chapter 7

Proverb of Fire 601
Satan can't snatch or take anything from God, and that's why you need to put your children in God's hands!

Proverb of Fire 602
Don't get good sex confused with a good relationship. Some women are lying next to the men who will someday take their lives, and the very cord Satan used to bind them was sex. Abstinence takes the intoxicating effects of an ungodly soul tie out of the picture so you can clearly hear from God regarding one another—and possibly save your own life.

Proverb of Fire 603
There is a difference between cleaving and clinging. You will cleave to your spouse, but if you get with the wrong person, they will cling to you out of fear and distrust.

Proverb of Fire 604
Sometimes, it's that step you haven't taken that's keeping you from reaching the place you've been praying for.

Proverb of Fire 605
A man's strength is not measured by how strong his arms are; it is measured by how strong his faith is. With that being said, women of God, stop running behind men who can hit other men, but can't touch a demon.

Proverb of Fire 606
Your exes are not your enemies. They are just friendly reminders that you can't give yourself away since you don't belong to you.

Proverb of Fire 607
Everything you get into is established on a foundation. Check the foundation, and you'll know if that thing is going to stand!

Proverb of Fire 608
Unforgiveness is a prison where the offended has become the offenders.

Proverb of Fire 609
If a divorced man says he's never getting married again, here's what he's really saying:

- I have not forgiven my ex.
- I'm living in fear of the uncertain, therefore, my faith is nonexistent.
- I generalize women. Because I was wronged by one woman, I'd rather judge the gender, rather than discern the spirits or even take accountability for my own choices.
- I plan to fornicate; I'm just not about to make it right in God's eyes.
- I don't truly fear God, and that's why it's easier for me to burn than it is for me to marry because I'll cool myself off on any woman who dares to call me her "boyfriend."
- The material possessions I have are more valuable to me than any woman, so out of fear of losing my stuff, I'd rather not even sign that contract we call a marriage certificate. Oh, but I will sign for a car note, pay rent, buy a home or invest in the things that are worthwhile to me, but I won't do that for you or any other woman.

- You're not even worth the skin you're in. Sure, I understand that fornicators won't enter heaven, but no worries. More than likely, I will have kicked you to the curb long before you're dead, so you'll have plenty of time to repent.
- I want to test drive you with no permit or license because I don't plan to buy you. I just wanna see how you drive and how long I can drive you before you end the test drive or you break down.
- I'm not gonna make a great father because I'm gonna teach my daughters that because they're women, they're worthless and predisposed to evil.
- The woman who hurt or upset me bad enough for me to come up with that decision is still the most important and most influential person in my life.

Proverb of Fire 610

The problem with a lot of us "grown" women is we get into relationships with guys who aren't mature enough to understand us, and then, we try to teach them our language. STOP IT! Your man of God speaks "you" fluently.

Proverb of Fire 611

Dear Prophet, If God gives you a word for somebody, you don't have to make it come true or convince them of it. You simply need to deliver it.
Dear Saints, If a prophet gives you a word, you don't have to make it come true. You simply need to obey God, and if that Word came from God, it will manifest in due season.
Stop trying to help God be God.

Proverb of Fire 612
Ladies, if a man will refrain from fornication because of his love and fear of God, he will refrain from adultery because of his love and fear of God. If he's not strong enough to resist temptation when he's not married to you, he won't be able to resist the sure-to-come temptation when he is married to you.

Proverb of Fire 613
Some people get upset when they're rejected by the wrong people. I don't. I get upset when they actually want to be a part of my life.

Proverb of Fire 614
If your heart was your face, how would you look?

Proverb of Fire 615
The cure for stress is to live each day in present tense, not past tense and not future tense—just live today for today, and let tomorrow's joys and sorrows meet you tomorrow! When you take each day one day at a time, you will forgive the pangs of yesterday and those who brought them to you, and you won't be anxious for tomorrow because you'll be too busy living in today! Today, you may not have enough money for that bill, but that doesn't mean that God won't bless you with it tomorrow. Today, you may not have the answers to the challenges you're facing, but tomorrow may be the day that God answers that problem for you and commands it to give up the wisdom stored in it. Today, your spouse may not be what you want him to be, but tomorrow may be the day that the Lord changes him. Stop living in yesterday and stop trying to figure out tomorrow—just take

life one day at a time, one prayer at a time, one problem at a time because there's one God who is above it all—and He doesn't like to be rushed.

Proverb of Fire 616
We have to live lives of full surrender to God! Whatever part of you that you refuse to surrender is the door the enemy will use to attack you.

Proverb of Fire 617
You can't serve the Devil and then call heaven and report the Devil when he starts acting like the Devil with you!

Proverb of Fire 618
Ladies, ain't nothing wrong with you telling yourself you're too good for the wrong man. I tell myself this truth all the time.

Proverb of Fire 619
This one is for the single women of God who keep searching for their own customizable Boaz's in the world. Did you know that the man you're trying to lead to Christ chose you from a dark place? The Bible tells us that the world walks in darkness; they are blind. Did you know that if that man was to get saved, sanctified and filled with the Holy Spirit, his eyes would open and he more than likely wouldn't be interested in you? Understand this: Sometimes, it's the sin, familiar spirits, and like mentalities that people have that draw them to one another. Once that mess is gone, the yoke breaks, the scabs fall off the eyes and people do make different choices, but this time, they do it with the lights on.

Proverb of Fire 620
A country never prepares for war during a war. A country prepares for war in times of peace. Marriage should be the same way. You don't look for solutions when the problems have arrived; you look to prevent the problems from arriving.

Proverb of Fire 621
If you depend on the prophet for a word, you will dry up. The prophet comes to confirm, rebuke and exhort; not to sustain you.

Proverb of Fire 622
Elevation is always preceded by manifestation! Anytime you're about to be taken from one realm and elevated to the next, the Devil will always reveal his hiding place, whether he's hiding out in your family, friendship circle or church! Stop getting mad at people and start focusing on where God is taking you!

Proverb of Fire 623
You have to look like the world to draw the world to you, BUT you have to look like Christ to draw the world to Jesus.

Proverb of Fire 624
A confused man's shelter is his opinion, but a wise man takes shelter in the wisdom of the Almighty God.

Proverb of Fire 625
I don't believe what people tell me; I believe what they show me.

Proverb of Fire 626
When you speak of your disease more than you speak of your Healer, you have the disease, but you have not allowed the Healer to have you. Speak the truth and the truth will cast out every lie that dares to inhabit your body!

Proverb of Fire 627
It is better to be alone and in peace than to be in the company of fools.

Proverb of Fire 628
You can't force God to accept the man you've chosen for yourself. Instead, He will let you flaunt that guy around until you come to the end of yourself and acknowledge that He was right all along.

Proverb of Fire 629
The lake of fire is the unrestrained fury of God poured out without measure.

Proverb of Fire 630
Anything and anyone you put before God is an idol.

Proverb of Fire 631
If you want to find where a stronghold is in your life, look for patterns.

Proverb of Fire 632
When God reads your life's story to the angels, is He telling a love story or a horror story? Know this: You are the one with the pen, but God is the one who will narrate, rate and file your story.

Proverb of Fire 633

The present version of you is always fighting with the better version of you. Get out of God's way so He can win that battle for you.

Proverb of Fire 634

A man who wants you more than life itself is a man who could easily kill you. Being some man's idol is never flattering; it's dangerous.

Proverb of Fire 635

Did you know that most ducks are monogamous for a year? The female will accept a male to be her mate, and he will follow her around and even stay by her side when she lays his eggs. But, after the eggs hatch and she becomes a mother, the male will get tired of her tending to them, and he will leave in search of another mate. When mating season is over, he hangs with the other male ducks until mating season commences. Then, there is a bird called a House Wren. These birds will pair up for a season, and while the male tends to the young, the female will often find another mate and start a family with him—only to leave him with their young. Finally, there's the albatross. This bird takes up to ten years to reach sexual maturity, and when it does, it sits amongst the elders for years learning the mating rituals. After it selects a mate, the two create their own way of communicating—they have children and they both stick around to raise them. The problem with today's society is that too many women are going after ducks and too many men are placing the word "house" on a wren. Learn from the albatross; it is patient and it seeks wise counsel before it pursues a mate. When you catch the wisdom of God, you will know when to duck.

Proverb of Fire 636
The bravest thing you can ever do is go against yourself. Satan's already defeated.

Proverb of Fire 637
Ignoring a stronghold won't make it go away. It has to be confronted, torn down, tread upon and it must settle as dust underneath your feet in order for you to get over it.

Proverb of Fire 638
A silent prayer is better than a loud rebuke.

Proverb of Fire 639
When you are a daughter of the Most High God, you are honored, meaning, you are crowned with the glory of God. You are your husband's crown (honor) and honor does not belong on a fool.

Proverb of Fire 640
To learn a new language, you must immerse yourself in the language of your choice. That's why Satan encourages people to listen to demonic music and watch flesh-provoking shows.

Proverb of Fire 641
Holiness isn't individually defined; it's the pure nature of God.

Proverb of Fire 642
Elevation takes one step at a time and it can't be rushed.

Proverb of Fire 643
If you are not hidden, you cannot be found.

Proverb of Fire 644
Of all the things you can lose in this life, do not lose your humility. It is one of the most beautiful assets that you have. When you're clothed in humility, you can change a chaotic atmosphere by simply smiling. When you're clothed in humility, you can win a war by saying nothing. When you're clothed in humility, you can have anything you want. I've worn pride; I've worn contention, but nothing I've ever worn has ever given me the results I've gotten when I've worn humility.

Proverb of Fire 645
You can't beat the Devil with religion. You have to hit him with the Word.

Proverb of Fire 646
Some people have loved and lost repeatedly because they keep falling in love with the lost.

Proverb of Fire 647
When a man tries to fornicate with you, he is admitting that he's not strong enough to resist temptation. In other words, he won't make a trustworthy husband. If God can't trust him, you can't trust him. Here's how that conversation should go: Dude with Fiery Loins: So, I was thinking of you today and I hope I don't offend you, but I want to make love to you. The Right Response: Okay, thank you. It was nice knowing you. Dude with Fiery Loins: Huh? Nice knowing me? You're breaking up with me? The Right Response: I appreciate your honesty; really, I do, but the position you have open is not

the one I was applying for, nor do I want to try and work my way up the ladder towards that position. I'm already qualified to be my husband's wife, but being some man's whore was not on my resume, nor am I interested in it. I would appreciate it if you didn't call me anymore.

Proverb of Fire 648
You can't break up with Satan if you're still in a relationship with sin. That's like telling a man that you don't want to be his wife anymore, but you do want to continue having sex with him.

Proverb of Fire 649
A woman who tries to lead a man into fornication has already proven that she doesn't do well in the submission arena.

Proverb of Fire 650
Revelation: Heaven doesn't play by your rules.

Proverb of Fire 651
A man who tries to lead you into fornication has already proven that he can't be trusted to lead his home because he's following the Devil with his flesh.

Proverb of Fire 652
A fornicating leader is a polluted well.

Proverb of Fire 653
Tapping into the heart of God is far better than tapping into His pocket.

Proverb of Fire 654

As a man thinks in his heart, so is he. You are what you think you are. If you think you're beautiful—you are! People will enjoy looking at you. If you think you're sexy—you are! And there are many lining up to have sex with you, but don't look for a wedding ring. If you think you're a wife— you are! And someone will come along and recognize that you are his wife! It starts on the inside and manifests on the outside!

Proverb of Fire 655

When you don't trust God, you'll move in your own strength, and that's when you'll find out how weak you really are.

Proverb of Fire 656

The next time someone has the audacity to be jealous of what God has done for you, ask them if they're willing to walk barefooted on that narrow, thorn-covered plank of a journey you had to walk. I believe folks with entitlement mindsets should be made to walk a hundred miles wearing the shoes of the people they're whining about.

Proverb of Fire 657

Don't let what you can see (people, situations, imaginations) distract you from what you cannot see (God working).

Proverb of Fire 658

Fornication is NOT an accident; it is ALWAYS premeditated. Now, you may say that you let that man come to your house, and you did not plan to fornicate with him, but subconsciously, you were open to let the chips fall as they may. Being abstinent means so much more than not having sex; it means to prepare yourself mentally and physically for the wait. In other words, you don't place yourself in situations where your flesh could speak louder than your convictions. Even if he came by unannounced, you didn't have to let him in. Stop calling fornication an accident, and seek to be delivered.

Proverb of Fire 659
Don't let someone who doesn't know the cost of your oil tell you how and where to use it.

Proverb of Fire 660
The same devils that tormented, robbed, manipulated and killed the people of God in 1819 are still here tormenting, robbing, manipulating and killing the people of God today. Don't get caught up in the "this is a new day" mentality. The elderly are full of wisdom because they've met the same devils who are out and about attacking and enticing people today. Open your ears and listen to them so you won't have to end up telling month-long stories about how life had to clock you across the head with the truth, and then, drag your unwilling body to a recovery room called "revelation."

Proverb of Fire 661
Some folks pray with you—and that's good. Some folks pray for you—and that's great. Some folks pray about you—and that's wise. Some folks pray against you—and that's when heaven and hell clash.

Proverb of Fire 662
There are no pretty people in hell. Everyone there looks like what they've been through.

Proverb of Fire 663
Love and lust cannot work together. They oppose one

another; they are at opposite ends of the spectrum. Though they may look and feel the same, they are at enmity with one another. Don't confuse the two and don't try to use one as a bridge to the other, because if you do, you will find out that those two bridges are not connected.

Proverb of Fire 664
Change never happens on the outside until it first occurs on the inside. What you see externally is a representative of what is going on internally.

Proverb of Fire 665
If Satan can cause a lion to think it's a kitten, he can intimidate it with his voice, but if a kitten believes that it's a lion, it can intimate Satan with its meow.

Proverb of Fire 666
Our problem is we are creatures of adaptation; we'll get into mindsets and stay there unless we're provoked by a storm to move. Sometimes, a storm is just a mental eviction notice.

Proverb of Fire 667
If God was to come back Sunday morning, a lot of folks would go to hell wearing their church shoes.

Proverb of Fire 668
Some folks go to secular concerts wearing diamond bracelets, but they go to church wearing their watches.

Proverb of Fire 669
The best part about not being where you want to be is having something to look forward to.

Proverb of Fire 670

You hug the Word with your heart, not with your body. You embrace the Word with your heart, not with your mouth. You witness the power of God through your obedience, not with your eyes. You touch the heart of God with your faith, not with your hands.

Proverb of Fire 671

Some of us are near-sighted saints, seeing only what's in our faces, but unable to see in the realm of the spirit. Some of us are far-sighted saints, being super spiritual, but can't see what's right in front of us. And then, some of us are blind—only led by what we feel.

Proverb of Fire 672

It's easy to get caught up complaining about what you don't have when you haven't learned to be thankful for what you do have. Always remember that there are plenty of people out there who would happily exchange problems with you any day. If they did, you'd really have something to complain about.

Proverb of Fire 673

A made-up mind is one the enemy can't breach.

Proverb of Fire 674

When you are married and you pray that God changes your spouse, what you'll notice is that He'll start to change you first. Why is this? It's because you noticed <u>your</u> issue in your spouse, therefore, to get the spouse to change, you need to grow into a new mindset; that way, you can no longer relate to the spouse in the old mindset. When you change your mind, your spouse can no longer walk with you since he is no longer in agreement with you in that area. When your spouse loves you, he will change his mind to continue to walk and relate to you.

Proverb of Fire 675
There is no such thing as an unanswered prayer. Sometimes, we just don't like God's response.

Proverb of Fire 676
Your flesh is Satan's most effective weapon against you. If you can get past yourself, you render Satan powerless in your life.

Proverb of Fire 677
If a thief broke in and stole your Bible, could the police prove it was yours by checking it for your fingerprints?

Proverb of Fire 678
Sometimes, Jesus will lead you into a person's life so that He can have a conversation with them through you. Don't interrupt their conversation to add your two cents. Just let Him use you.

Proverb of Fire 679
The Devil can pretend to be an angel of light, but his lack of genuine love betrays him every time.

Proverb of Fire 680
Heaven's most noted marriage complaints come from people who are married to their own reflections and don't like what they see.

Proverb of Fire 681
Satan's promises are lies laced with diluted truths. Never trust an angel who was stupid enough to get kicked out of heaven.

Proverb of Fire 682
A religious soul and a dead soul have one thing in common: they aren't going anywhere unless God calls them out of their pits.

Proverb of Fire 683
Love is not heart-shaped; your heart is shaped by your love or your lack thereof. Your heart was formed in love, deformed by sin and transformed by the renewing of your mind.

Proverb of Fire 684
You are the impossible made possible by God. If God can create you, why would you think there's anything too hard for Him? Believe.

Proverb of Fire 685
Faith and fear cannot co-exist. Doubt and faith cannot work together.

Proverb of Fire 686
Sometimes, the most faithful and effective prayers going up for you are coming from people you didn't even know were praying for you.

Proverb of Fire 687
Ishmael is a weapon formed against your purpose, your womb, your legacy and your relationship with God. Don't let

him prosper!

Proverb of Fire 688
Have you embraced this new place you're in or are you still standing there looking at the doorknob?

Proverb of Fire 689
No one ever said the journey would be easy, but we are assured that it's worth it.

Proverb of Fire 690
Sometimes, the distance between you and your blessing is as small as your mouth but as big as your words.

Proverb of Fire 691
The truth can only be heard by those who have ears and are willing to hear what the Spirit of the Lord is saying.

Proverb of Fire 692
In the midst of her losses, her pain, and her uncertainties, Ruth had no idea that God was going to bless her. She did not know that God was going to use her story to minister to generations of men and women across the globe. Her lines weren't rehearsed, nor was her story scripted. Her story made way for a testimony that would echo through time to be heard by you and me. Don't think that God can't use you or your story. Sometimes, an opposition is nothing but a force getting you in position to be used by God.

Proverb of Fire 693
God won't hand you the keys to your new place until you vacate the old mindset.

Proverb of Fire 694
If you're willing to put God ahead of yourself in every area of your life, God is going to use you mightily. If you hate sin, you are in one accord with God. If you can stand up against ridicule, persecution, religiousness, and false leaders, God is going to use you as a Joshua for your generation!

Proverb of Fire 695
You can't discount a woman who knows her worth.

Proverb of Fire 696
If wisdom was meat for your bones, how many of us would be malnourished? Some folks would've died from starvation a long time ago.

Proverb of Fire 697
Marrying Satan won't get him into heaven on a fiancé visa. In heaven, there are no green cards.

Proverb of Fire 698
The problem with the average believer is they believe in God, but they don't believe Him. This means they know of God, but they don't truly know Him.

Proverb of Fire 699
Unequally yoked equals spiritual pedophilia.

Proverb of Fire 700
Sex, for a lost soul, is currency designed to buy what he or she is not trusting God for.

Chapter 8

Proverb of Fire 701
Understand this—when the enemy is trying to get your attention, he's trying to distract you from something. Keep your eyes stayed on God. Don't give your attention to seducing or distracting spirits because they've come to get your attention for a reason.

Proverb of Fire 702
Some people measure themselves by the level, status, and titles of their friends, but a wise man knows that his enemies are a reflection of his rank. When the Devil sends imps after you, it's because of your low rank, but when he starts sending his high-ranking devils after you, it's because you are a real threat to his kingdom.

Proverb of Fire 703
What you are called to is greater than what you've been called away from.

Proverb of Fire 704
Too many saints have Satan as their "sugar-daddy" as if God ought to be satisfied because He's the main one. No! God has to be the only God you serve, otherwise, he will spit you out of His mouth, and then, officiate the wedding between you and your side of Satan. That marriage would last an eternity.

Proverb of Fire 705
Truth be told, there is no such thing as "crazy," but there is such a thing as "demon-possessed."

Proverb of Fire 706
A prophet in unrepentant fornication doubles as a witch.

Proverb of Fire 707
To fornicate means to openly invite death into your body in exchange for a few minutes of pleasure.

Proverb of Fire 708
There is no such thing as a spiritual bail out. True repentance draws God's forgiveness, but it does not exempt you from His already declared Word. So, for example, if you fornicate and catch a disease as a result of your fornication, true repentance will draw God's forgiveness, but it won't make the consequences (disease and soul ties) go away. It would only mean that the disease and soul ties no longer have rights to kill you, but they can attack at will until you get enough faith to be free of them. Just stay in God's will, and you won't have to spend years trying to undo what you've done in a moment's time.

Proverb of Fire 709
You are either Satan's dream come true or his worst nightmare.

Proverb of Fire 710
The greatest distance between you and your God-ordained husband is the equivalent of the distance between you and God. In other words, if sin is separating you from God, sin is separating you from the blessings of God.

Proverb of Fire 711
It is better to submit to the truth than it is to be humbled by it.

Proverb of Fire 712
Trying to change a man is like trying to tame a rattlesnake.

Proverb of Fire 713
Evil imaginations are nothing but demon commercials. Don't sit there and watch that mess, or you may end up buying the lies. Change the channel.

Proverb of Fire 714
Being sexually compatible with someone is the least of your worries. You'd better make sure you're spiritually compatible (equally yoked), otherwise, you may find yourself married to someone who is good at uncovering you naturally, but does not have the knowledge or capacity to cover you spiritually.

Proverb of Fire 715
If the slave girl with the spirit of divination was alive today, she would likely be an ordained prophetess in somebody's church.

Proverb of Fire 716
Sin cuts off the circulation to your blessings.

Proverb of Fire 717
There will be many people who will wish for your downfall, pray for your demise, weep when you're laughing, laugh when you're weeping and frown at the sound of your name. We call them enemies, but God calls them footstools.

Proverb of Fire 718
Faith is unlimited restriction based on what God said. It is the ability to move natural things with the spirit of truth.

Proverb of Fire 719
Just because a man says "amen" doesn't make him a Christian. Don't rush to the altar with the first guy you see

wearing church shoes.

Proverb of Fire 720
If you spend tomorrow regretting today, you will always be a slave of yesterday.

Proverb of Fire 721
A fact is man's version of the truth, but it is always discredited and dismissed. The truth is Jesus Christ, and even though many have attempted to discredit Him, He cannot be dismissed. He simply is and was and will always be.

Proverb of Fire 722
You can take him to church, but you can't take him to the King.

Proverb of Fire 723
If you marry a broken man, he's going to:
- Break your heart.
- Break your soul.
- Cause you to break up with reality.

Don't get mad at him. He's only being what he is: broken.

Proverb of Fire 724
Your plans for you are cute, but God's plans for you are established.

Proverb of Fire 725
Operating in fear is like wrapping a huge boa constrictor around your neck, and then, attempting to tickle it. Walk in faith.

Proverb of Fire 726

Sometimes, we make plans for ourselves that don't match God's plans for us, and then, we find ourselves in situations that we mislabel as "trials" because we stand by helplessly and watch God's plans override our own. That's not a trial; it's simply a showdown of our plans versus God's plans, and we know how that ends.

Proverb of Fire 727

Closed doors are designed to keep something or someone out.

Proverb of Fire 728

People who love sin hate righteousness and those who love righteousness hate sin.

Proverb of Fire 729

If you define your worth by the people in your life and the possessions you have, you have labeled yourself as worthless.

Proverb of Fire 730

Be angry, but sin not. People are going to offend you, but get over it so you can get past it as fast as possible. One of the most common attacks of the enemy is to offend you and preoccupy your mind with what someone did to you, said about you or didn't do for you so that you'll lose focus on your God-given assignment. When Satan starts harassing you, he is attempting to distract you. If he is successful, he will then slither right past you and begin to attack the blessings he sees in front of you. Offense is a part of life. Shake it off and move forward. The worst thing you can do to someone who is on demonic assignment is to cause them to get a failing grade on their assignment!

Proverb of Fire 731
Kissing before marriage is like heating up an oven, even though you know you're not gonna put anything in it.

Proverb of Fire 732
If God was to catch you and pat you down today, what would He find in your heart? Would He find pride, idolatry, bitterness, strife, lust, perversion, or envy? Would He find gossip between your teeth, lies under your tongue, blood on your hands or have you hidden your sins in more private areas? There is no place that you can hide from God! Let Him find you with love in your heart, blessings on your lips, charity in your hands and holiness as your cloak.

Proverb of Fire 733
It is better to be married to the one who sees you than it is to be married to the one who looks at you.

Proverb of Fire 734
God's least plans for you are better than your greatest plans for yourself. It's okay to plan big, but it's better to hand your plans over to the Lord and let Him upgrade them.

Proverb of Fire 735
Stop making yourself available to unavailable people.

Proverb of Fire 736
A married man was in the hotel with his mistress when death came to collect his soul. A brawling woman was halfway through a fight with another brawling woman when death came to collect her soul. A lawyer was in the middle of a lie

when death came to collect his soul. A prostitute was earning her wages when death came to collect her soul. A politician was in the middle of being a politician when death came to collect his soul. Salvation is for TODAY! It's not something you should put off to enjoy a few more years of sin! After all, sin is a bridge that allows death to cross the spiritual gulf between Hades and mankind. Don't let sin build a bridge in your life!

Proverb of Fire 737
The most amazing testimony that you have today is that you are alive! If you can breathe, you can testify.

Proverb of Fire 738
How are you going to handle being hated for His name's sake if you complain every time you come across someone who doesn't like you?

Proverb of Fire 739
The power to change that situation is in your belly and has to flow out of your mouth! Speak the Word and stop crying!

Proverb of Fire 740
Satan can't stop what God has set in motion.

Proverb of Fire 741
Fear moves the Devil, but faith removes him.

Proverb of Fire 742
Fornicators are illegally united as one person (married) to the person or people they've fornicated with. In other words, they are married, but their unions don't have God's blessing.

Proverb of Fire 743
Every true-to-life story is comprised of a main character, a villain and a hero. In your life, you are your main character and your villain is whoever or whatever is opposing you. Sometimes, your villain is you.

Proverb of Fire 744
You can never learn to speak the language of understanding if you are a foreigner to knowledge.

Proverb of Fire 745
A person's perception of you isn't always a mirrored reflection of your character. In most cases, it is a magnified reflection of their own hearts or strongholds.

Proverb of Fire 746
Never get so blinded by the appearance of a man's flesh that you fail to see his spirit.

Proverb of Fire 747
Pride is weakness masquerading as strength.

Proverb of Fire 748
Wealth without wisdom is a snare.

Proverb of Fire 749
Holiness makes you irresistible to God. It makes Him want to shower you with blessings because you are radiating a beauty that only spiritual eyes can see, a beauty that only wisdom can appreciate.

Proverb of Fire 750
Debt attracts more debt. Release it.

Proverb of Fire 751

If you're not stepping forward, you're stepping backward. If you're not standing up, you're sitting down. If you're not going to heaven, you're going to hell. Contrary to popular belief, there is no in between!

Proverb of Fire 752

The right man will guard your purity without you asking him to do so.

Proverb of Fire 753

Wherever there is fear, there is failure. Wherever there is faith, there is the evidence thereof.

Proverb of Fire 754

Courtships don't require the amount of time that dating requires since, in courtship, both parties agree that the purpose of the courtship is marriage if God confirms that He has led them to one another. Dating is a guessing game where people play musical chairs with one another's souls.

Proverb of Fire 755

Love is your spiritual bank account and faith is your pin number. If you don't have faith, you can't withdraw from the Word.

Proverb of Fire 756

Find your fears and slaughter them. It is only then that you'll be able to move beyond your current reality into your destiny.

Proverb of Fire 757

Your husband can't find you until you've found yourself.

Who you are is hidden deep within the heart of God.
Seek His heart and you'll find you.

Proverb of Fire 758
You can't wear the uniform of righteousness while cheering
for the Devil's team.

Proverb of Fire 759
Never ever get so caught up in your opportunity to be liked
by a person that you disregard the fact that you are loved by
God.

Proverb of Fire 760
Marrying a blind man won't make him see.

Proverb of Fire 761
Some women delay the arrival of the husbands God wants to
send to them because they are off in some dark corner
kissing on the ones that Satan sent.

Proverb of Fire 762
Wisdom is free for the taking, but understanding will cost
you everything. Why is that? With faith, you just believe and
obey the Lord, but to get understanding, you first have to get
knowledge. Once you take from the tree of knowledge, you
are accountable for your choices, so you'll need
understanding to keep you from making those wrong choices
again. When Adam and Eve sinned, they had to be given the
understanding of what they'd done wrong before they were
sent out of the Garden. They wanted the knowledge of good
and evil and they got it, but it cost them everything.

Proverb of Fire 763
Don't let anyone silence your anointing.

Proverb of Fire 764
Any man who's willing to cheat with you has already cheated on you. In the game of adultery, the real loser is the one who gets the guy. After all, you can't win a loser.

Proverb of Fire 765
You are a cup that's being filled everyday. You will pour out whatever you've been allowing into you. That's why you shouldn't trust a secular Christian.

Proverb of Fire 766
Religiousness is the short bus headed to hell. Holiness is the flight you don't want to miss.

Proverb of Fire 767
If someone tries to hold you to your past, cut them out of your future. Some people find themselves not being able to move forward into tomorrow because yesterday has a leash on them and somebody they love is holding it.

Proverb of Fire 768
True prophets don't always tell you what you want to hear, they tell you what you need to hear. On that note, beware of prophets who always give you candy but no meat.

Proverb of Fire 769
To Satan, you're nothing more than an opportunity for him to get even with the Lord.

Proverb of Fire 770
People say the truth is mean, but people in hell could tell you that hell is meaner.

Proverb of Fire 771
The problem with the traditional church is that it's traditional. God didn't create you to follow a list of man-made rules. He said to be led by His Spirit.

Proverb of Fire 772
A loveless marriage is like a godless church.

Proverb of Fire 773
Your depth of understanding is measured by the width of your knowledge.

Proverb of Fire 774
Offer God the best of who you are, and He will show you the rest of who you are. Believe it or not, you are a vault that only the Word of God can unlock. Don't waste your time chasing the valueless things of the world when your most valuable treasure is locked away in your heart.

Proverb of Fire 775
You can't sex your way into a blessing, but you can sex your way out of one.

Proverb of Fire 776
The truth is potent enough to destroy a lie and silence a liar.

Proverb of Fire 777
If you don't value yourself enough to remain pure, you're gonna attract defiled men who need to further defile you to

make themselves feel valuable.

Proverb of Fire 778
An unchanged mind is the Devil's workstation.

Proverb of Fire 779
Sin is a wild and merciless beast that wants to devour you whole. Grace is the love of God holding that beast back after you have mocked it and opened its gate. Mercy is God holding Himself back from giving you what you deserve. Love is God seeing Christ in you and giving you what He deserves.

Proverb of Fire 780
Some marriages are nothing more than sex circuses where clowns come to perform while wearing masks, but when the costumes come off, the show is over!

Proverb of Fire 781
We often get friendly people confused with friends.

Proverb of Fire 782
Once you taste and see that the Lord is good, Satan has nothing left to offer you.

Proverb of Fire 783
You can't force the Lord to submit to your plans for the life He has given you. Instead, your plans will eventually turn around and confess that God was right all along.

Proverb of Fire 784
Sometimes, you give a platform to your enemies by addressing them. Stop it. Never address the person. Address the demon driving or influencing the person.

Proverb of Fire 785
Hollywood has tainted so many of you to the point where you can't see who you are because you're blinded by who you're trying to be. Turn the television off for a while and discover the hidden beauty of your design; that way, you'll offer your husband the best of who you are and not a counterfeit version of another woman. Be you and any man who doesn't like the real you is clearly not your God-appointed husband anyway.

Proverb of Fire 786
Wisdom is free, but foolishness can cost you your life.

Proverb of Fire 787
God always reveal the heart of a man by lifting up the people around him whom he claims to love. Saul loved David until he found out that David was anointed to take his place.

Proverb of Fire 788
Gossips are the Devil's tools. Their assignment is to keep others from testifying by making them ashamed of their testimonies, but when you testify, you take away the gossip's job.

Proverb of Fire 789
Turn on the lights when a man is hung over and he will curse at you. A rebellious man has the same reaction when you are a light and you get too close to him.

Proverb of Fire 790
Peter and Paul didn't compete because they had Christ in common.

Proverb of Fire 791

Thinking love is an emotion is one of the main reasons marriages fail today. Love is not an emotion. Emotions change, but love never fails. On average, most people marry out of emotions, and that's why divorce attorneys rake in a lot of money. Love is a spirit; it is the very heart of who God is. Love never fails, nor does it change. One of the easiest ways to see if you "have feelings" for someone as opposed to loving them is to ask yourself this pointed question: If the man I'm seeing were to have an accident, become disfigured and lose his ability to contribute financially to our household, would I stick around? Love would stick around, but someone with feelings would have a change of heart and leave. Love never fails, but people do.

Proverb of Fire 792

Fornication never involves just two people. When people join themselves in rebellion, Satan is in their midst. But when two people are gathered in the name of the Lord, He is in the midst.

Proverb of Fire 793

The spirit of a person draws love because our spirits are eternal just as love is eternal, but the flesh draws lust because the flesh is temporary just as lust is temporary.

Proverb of Fire 794

People who try to understand spiritual things with their carnal minds often end up frustrated.

Proverb of Fire 795

You can't sleep with a man you are not married to and then, expect God to pay your bills. The minute you lie down with a man, he is responsible for you in God's eyes because he is now your husband—although illegally! If you're sexually active and struggling, you literally let Satan screw you over— twice! Sex comes after marriage, not before it.

Proverb of Fire 796
A woman who gets her husband through fornication is a woman who needs to have a marriage counselor, a pastor and a good attorney on speed dial.

Proverb of Fire 797
Think about that one guy you dated who was the "love of your life." Would you date him now? If so, your mind hasn't been renewed.

Proverb of Fire 798
Purpose and position go hand-in-hand. What good am I if my purpose is to build houses in Israel, but I'm off in Egypt somewhere?

Proverb of Fire 799
The difference between a Christian victim and a Christian overcomer is knowledge.

Proverb of Fire 800
Without Goliath, David wouldn't have seen promotion, so why are you running from your giants?

Chapter 9

Proverb of Fire 801

Sometimes, the answers to your prayers aren't found in your many words; it's found in your hour of silence. We ask God many questions, but how many of us are listening to Him for a response?

Proverb of Fire 802

To an unbelieving man, you are a mystery. There is something fascinating about you and an unbeliever wants to figure out this great mystery. He wants to take you out, spend time with you, spend money on you and maybe even meet you at the altar. The happiest time you will have with him is when he hasn't yet figured you out, but once the mystery is solved, and he realizes he can't connect with you the way he connected with an unbelieving woman, he's going to leave. It's not that you're a bad woman or you've done some great evil to him; the problem is he can't walk with you since the two of you don't agree. How can he agree with you when the two of you don't even serve the same God? How can he continue to live with you after he's had his fill of you, and realizes there is nothing else to you that he can connect with? After you submit yourself to an ungodly man, you are no different to him than an ungodly woman and he will treat you as such.

Proverb of Fire 803

The Lord has set the price for your hand at a rate that only your God-appointed husband can afford. Don't discount yourself for anyone.

Proverb of Fire 804

To pray means to communicate with God, but it's your faith

that gives Him an open line to respond to you.

Proverb of Fire 805
Let the guy lead the courtship. That way, you'll see which direction he is taking you in.

Proverb of Fire 806
Beware of people who only show up when your joy has left. Miserable people can smell misery from a "smile" away.

Proverb of Fire 807
A man who is exposed to the enemy cannot cover a woman! He can marry her, but he can't cover her, seeing that he himself is exposed.

Proverb of Fire 808
False humility is pride masquerading as love.

Proverb of Fire 809
Ruth did not position herself to be found by Boaz; Ruth followed Jewish tradition because she loved her mother-in-law. She didn't want to leave Naomi, and she knew the only way to stick around was to follow their tradition. Naomi offered Ruth and Orpah the opportunities to go back to their lands and follow their own gods, but Ruth wasn't interested in Naomi's initial offer. She wanted to stay there and raise up children for her deceased husband. Nowadays, women run out and throw themselves in front of men and they use Ruth's story to justify their behavior. Nevertheless, to be a modern day Ruth, you would have to go back under the law which Christ delivered you from. The way to position yourself to be found nowadays is to simply seek the Kingdom of God and all its righteousness. God said that in finding you,

a husband would obtain favor from Him. This is because your husband has to stay in Him to find you, therefore, both of you are in His will. But when you have to put yourself out there to be found, it's because the person you are trying to be found by isn't looking for you or looking at you the right way. Sadly enough, many women have to get these lessons from the belt of fire called "experience" because they see what they want and pursue it as opposed to seeing the Word they need and pursuing Him. Your husband will find you in Christ, and you won't have to wear an extra layer of eyeliner or baptize your lips in lipstick to attract him.

Proverb of Fire 810
If you don't crucify the lusts of the flesh, they will turn around and crucify you!

Proverb of Fire 811
When the truth stands up, the Devil takes a seat.

Proverb of Fire 812
The Devil isn't scared of you going to church; he's afraid of you realizing that you are the church.

Proverb of Fire 813
For some people, being right is more important than the truth.

Proverb of Fire 814
A husband worth waiting for won't mind waiting.

Proverb of Fire 815
Satan extended an opportunity for me to be a victim, but I passed it up because God extended an opportunity for me to

be more than a conqueror through Christ Jesus. That position actually pays more, plus, it has benefits.

Proverb of Fire 816
Don't compete for a man and don't fight over a man. A man worth fighting for won't have you fighting.

Proverb of Fire 817
Never settle for a man who thinks he's settling for you.

Proverb of Fire 818
People who fit in move with the crowd, but people who stand out cause the crowd to move.

Proverb of Fire 819
Praying means you want answers. Complaining and gossiping means you've already answered yourself.

Proverb of Fire 820
The most powerful and effective sermons you'll ever preach are to yourself.

Proverb of Fire 821
Irony: Sometimes, people sin for years trying to get to something God would have blessed them with within months had they been faithful to Him.

Proverb of Fire 822
In many parts of the world, there are people who are considered uncivilized because they live off the land and have no established governments. They wear the skins of animals and they hunt their own food. If you were to walk up to a tribe of people who have not been tainted or tempted

by the cares of this world, and you were to hand them a bucket of diamonds, they'd probably toss them back at you. To them, a diamond is nothing but a worthless rock. To us, a diamond represents so much more. The same goes for the wrong man versus the right man. If you give yourself to the wrong man, he won't know how to love you because, in his world, you are worthless. To him, you're just another woman. To him, you are common. Nevertheless, the right man will see your value, and he will treat you like the precious diamond you are. To him, you are no ordinary woman. To him, you are uncommon. To him, you are worth his last name. He will love you, protect you, and most of all, God has determined that he has paid the price for you—that price being: faithfulness, obedience, and perseverance. It's up to you. Will you settle for the man who sees you as just another woman or will you wait for the one who has the receipt for your heart?

Proverb of Fire 823
Oftentimes, it's what Satan promises to give you that ends up becoming the thing that he's keeping you from.

Proverb of Fire 824
Here's how I measure opinions: I create a mental balance scale and I place people's opinions of me on one side, and then, I place my salvation, bills and what God says about me on the other side. That scale hasn't moved yet.

Proverb of Fire 825
When I died to myself and the new me arose, I had to leave that which I was familiar with because they could no longer recognize me. In other words, I became a stranger in my own

home.

Proverb of Fire 826
You can "make moves" without God, but you won't go anywhere.

Proverb of Fire 827
A man who takes you to the altar just because he wants to have unlimited sex with you is the same man who'll send you back to the altar just because he wants to have unlimited sex with someone else.

Proverb of Fire 828
Fornication is a thief's ladder designed to help him reach women he spiritually can't afford.

Proverb of Fire 829
Sometimes, folks aren't attracted to types of people; they are unknowingly attracted to familiar spirits. That's why they date the same devils behind different faces.

Proverb of Fire 830
A fool with many words is confused by silence.

Proverb of Fire 831
Some people wrestle with real problems. Others wrestle with themselves because they are the problem.

Proverb of Fire 832
A simple man is affected by his past, whereas, a wise man is inspired by his.

Proverb of Fire 833
Every man of God is not your man of God. God will only grant one man permission to have your hand. Only one man is your God-ordained husband. Everyone else would only be auditioning to be your ex-husband.

Proverb of Fire 834
Broken glass often hurts the people who try to clean it up. Broken people often hurt the people who try to clean them up.

Proverb of Fire 835
The simple truth is too complicated for a fool.

Proverb of Fire 836
There's a difference between a man who wants to get married and a man who desires to be a husband.

Proverb of Fire 837
Don't waste your wisdom on people who don't know its value.

Proverb of Fire 838
Familiar people will always question the call on your life because it does not reflect the direction they thought you'd go in.

Proverb of Fire 839
You can't wear summer shoes in the winter! You have to dress for the season you're in, otherwise, you may die from exposure!

Proverb of Fire 840
You can never be the right woman for the wrong man, so stop trying.

Proverb of Fire 841
There are levels in the realm of the spirit, and some of those levels require you to have little to no baggage. Cast ALL of your burdens on Christ Jesus so you can receive your promotion.

Proverb of Fire 842
Having a Bible that you rarely read is like walking to work when you have a car.

Proverb of Fire 843
Sex is the currency in an ungodly relationship, but it can never afford true love.

Proverb of Fire 844
Calling God when you're in sin and under attack is like robbing the bank with your friend, and then, calling the police because that friend has robbed you. When you call on the name of the Lord, you do it because you want to get out of the sin, not because you're not getting out of the sin what you want from it.

Proverb of Fire 845
Many of you are living horrible lives because you've joined ministries that God did not tell you to join. You joined them out of religiousness, but had you prayed, the Lord would've told you that He was not in those buildings. Ask the Lord to send you where His Spirit is, otherwise, you may end up in an empty building full of empty shells who look to empty

leaders to be filled.

Proverb of Fire 846
I know you've thought about how much of a blessing your husband is going to be to you, but have you ever stopped to ask yourself if you'd be a blessing to your husband outside of sex and a home cooked meal? The answer could help you understand why his arrival has been delayed if it's been delayed.

Proverb of Fire 847
Love never fails, but lust has an expiration date.

Proverb of Fire 848
A changed mind equals a changed life.

Proverb of Fire 849
Lust isn't always sexual. Lust means to have an ungodly desire for something.

Proverb of Fire 850
You don't have the potential to be great—you are great! You simply have the potential to fail, and unfortunately, many people have successfully failed at being who they were designed to be.

Proverb of Fire 851
God is love, and it is impossible for Him to tell a lie. Satan is the author of a lie, but it's not impossible for him to tell the truth. In other words, there is no such thing as a lie told in love since it can't be told by love. The word "white lie" is a lie itself.

Proverb of Fire 852
Whatever problems you may be facing, always remember, there is someone out there with greater problems who'd be happy to trade places with you.

Proverb of Fire 853
Having a baby with an ungodly man is like starting a business with a junkie.

Proverb of Fire 854
Faith and fear are fraternal twins. Even though they are birthed in the same womb (our hearts), they look nothing alike.

Proverb of Fire 855
It ain't faith until religious folks think you need deliverance or a straight-jacket.

Proverb of Fire 856
Beware of friends who always need something from you, but never give you anything but a conversation in return.

Proverb of Fire 857
Women of God, don't let a man uncover you in the natural before he covers you in the spirit.

Proverb of Fire 858
Who is the wrong man or woman to you romantically? A pause button on your destiny, an abort button on your blessings, a destruction button on your peace, and a fast forward button on your life. Wait on God.

Proverb of Fire 859
If there is anyone in your ear telling you that all men are cheaters, you need to correct that person, and then, take a safe distance from them. Sometimes, women ask God for husbands and get delayed because they have some woman in their circle who keeps vomiting on their hearts. Esther was massaged with perfumed oils for six months to detoxify her and give her a pleasant scent, but many women today have been massaged with lies for so long that they stink with unforgiveness. These same women can't seem to understand why the king refuses to see them.

Proverb of Fire 860
If you don't love you, you cannot and will not embrace the love that God has for you. Self-rejection always starts with a person rejecting what God says and feels about them to embrace what others say about them.

Proverb of Fire 861
Satan's favorite weapon to use against you is a person whose opinion you value the most.

Proverb of Fire 862
You are a member of whatever you involve yourself in, including gossip. Don't be found in the wrong congregation.

Proverb of Fire 863
Here's the thing about good men. They are hard to find because YOU WERE NEVER SUPPOSED TO BE LOOKING FOR THEM! Just like God hides His faithful daughters in the Lord, He hides His faithful sons; that way, His children find each other by faith and not by sight.

Proverb of Fire 864
Every David has a Saul and every Joseph has green-eyed siblings.

Proverb of Fire 865
The Word of God covers your spirit man in layers. One layer of wisdom prepares you for the next layer of truth. You can't jump into revelation knowledge if you haven't acquired basic knowledge. Respect the process!

Proverb of Fire 866
Here's the truth. Every David needs a Goliath in order to be promoted. That's why Hollywood capitalizes on the villain versus the victor strategy. They draw you into a story of someone who's like you or similar to someone you know, and then, they present a problem to you. You watch as the victor struggles to overcome his or her villains, and then, the story ends once the victor wins and gets his or her due promotion. Did you know that people live this way as well? Every person alive has a Goliath, and sometimes, when a person is not currently engaged in battle with a Goliath or that person doesn't know who his or her giant is, they will go out and create issues with people. They consciously or sub-consciously do this just so they can have something or someone to overcome. Sometimes, these people come to you wearing the "friend" title, but they are not your friends; they are blind soldiers who've walked off the battlefield in search of their Goliaths. Sometimes, they are distant family members who suddenly try to reconnect with you. If you stick around long enough, they'll finally challenge you to battle, call on the name of the Lord and attempt to overcome you. Stop being flattered by people's words to you

and start examining their hearts toward you and others. You would be amazed at how many battles could have been avoided if you had only checked the fruit of the person.

Proverb of Fire 867
A man's fruit will always find him in his garden and overtake him.

Proverb of Fire 868
Faith goes where fear is too scared to go.

Proverb of Fire 869
Submission: Your husband is or will be your king, but Jesus is or should be your King of kings.

Proverb of Fire 870
One fake friend is more dangerous than one hundred real enemies.

Proverb of Fire 871
We often say to our spouses, "If you love me, you'll be faithful to me." Guess what? God says the same thing to us. We understand faithfulness when our hearts are involved, but it's a foreign concept when the shoe is on the other foot. That's why God says, "If you love Me, keep My commandments."

Proverb of Fire 872
You can't break up with sin when it still has a key to your heart.

Proverb of Fire 873
A man who marries to fulfill his lustful cravings is a man

who'll end up divorced because of his lustful cravings for other women. Marriage isn't the cure for lust because lust doesn't die when someone gets married.

Proverb of Fire 874
Unity divides the real from the fake, but division unites your enemies.

Proverb of Fire 875
In order to get the husband that you want, you have to be the wife that he needs.

Proverb of Fire 876
You can never have true obedience to God without love, therefore, anyone who follows the instructions of God because they want something from Him is not being obedient; they're being manipulative.

Proverb of Fire 877
The biggest battle we'll ever fight is against ourselves.

Proverb of Fire 878
Never remove yourself from God's hands to hand yourself to sin because if you do, sin will chew you up and spit out your bones. The worst part of it is that most people being consumed are so busy being entertained by their sinful thoughts and all that's going on around them that they don't realize the crunching they hear is their souls being crushed.

Proverb of Fire 879
One of the quickest ways to get yourself judged by the "traditional" church and the world is by being obedient to God. God opposes the traditions of men, and men with

traditions are strangers to holiness.

Proverb of Fire 880
Sex outside of a godly marriage is sex outside of God's protection. Demons don't respect condoms.

Proverb of Fire 881
I never believe a person's words; I believe their fruit.

Proverb of Fire 882
What I love about God is that He will take you and lift you above man's opinion of you.

Proverb of Fire 883
Lies will drive you into the arms of the wrong people, but the truth will chase you away from them.

Proverb of Fire 884
A seductive saint is a believer who hasn't been all the way through the fire.

Proverb of Fire 885
Because God had Samuel anoint Saul as king of Israel, Saul could not be deposed. You see, whenever God declares you as something, you will be that for the rest of your life because God's Word cannot and will never return to Him void. Nevertheless, that doesn't mean He will work through you. Saul remained king even after God left him, but he became a king with a reprobate mind. In other words, don't esteem the position; check the fruit!

Proverb of Fire 886
Satan isn't your only enemy. He is your number one enemy,

but there is another enemy that has direct access to you, and he uses this enemy to trip you up and bring you down. This enemy knows your plans, your deepest and darkest secrets, your weaknesses, and your strengths. This enemy is called your flesh.

Proverb of Fire 887
Anyone who offers to prophesy to you for money is a witch or a misguided prophet prostituting himself or herself for gain.

Proverb of Fire 888
You are empowered to succeed. You are empowered to overcome. You are empowered to survive. Empowered means the power has been placed within you. In other words, you have to tap in to keep from tapping out.

Proverb of Fire 889
I love God because He first loved me. I hate sin because it first hated me.

Proverb of Fire 890
It is easier to teach a whale to fly than it is to save a sinner who loves his or her sin. In other words, you can't "convince" anyone to love and follow the Lord; they have to want Him.

Proverb of Fire 891
God's love is too wonderful to be understood or analyzed. It can only be embraced.

Proverb of Fire 892
Be still and know that YAHWEH is God. He will be your Redeemer if you honor Him. He will be your Healer if you let

Him. He will be your Provider if you trust Him. He will be your Protector if you obey Him. He will be your God if you love Him.

Proverb of Fire 893
If you go into sin, you're going to come out with a sinner.

Proverb of Fire 894
Every bad situation is an opportunity for God to show you how good He is.

Proverb of Fire 895
When your day seems gloomy, look to Jesus for He is the light of the world.

Proverb of Fire 896
Pride says, "What about me?" Love says, "What about us?"

Proverb of Fire 897
A diamond ring is powerless against a demon. A marriage certificate is worthless to a bill collector. A husband should be able to cover and provide for his family. Don't be so anxious to get married that you end up with a married man. There is a difference between a married man and a husband.

Proverb of Fire 898
Valuable means you're able to be appraised or valued. Invaluable means there is nothing in this world that can measure your worth. The problem today is many people get married to folks who value them; that is, until they see something they think is worth more. Wait for the one who recognizes that there isn't a thing in this world worth losing you for.

Proverb of Fire 899
The Holy Spirit is the best accountability partner one can ever have.

Proverb of Fire 900
Where you are is not who you are unless you allow it to define you.

Chapter 10

Chapter 10

Proverb of Fire 901
Where there is no war, there is no victory.

Proverb of Fire 902
Dear Unbeliever,
The worst time to discover that God actually does exist is when you're standing in front of Him on Judgment Day.

Proverb of Fire 903
Oftentimes, what keeps money from coming into your life is your unwillingness to let money go out of your life. If you don't like your financial situation, sow until you do.

Proverb of Fire 904
A man will always offer you what he thinks you're worth. If he offers you his body, he's pretty much saying you deserve to be in sin, without a covering. In other words, he's discounting you in the natural because he can't afford you in the spirit.

Proverb of Fire 905
Many words are spoken against you, but none of those words have power until you believe them.

Proverb of Fire 906
Of all the valuable things we could give to God, the one thing He wants the most is what many people refuse to give Him: their hearts.

Proverb of Fire 907
Your struggles aren't for you; they are for someone else. You just have to get over yourself so you can deliver the message to them.

Proverb of Fire 908
Some people are miserable and content at the same time. Why? Misery is their own personal country and they've adapted to it while learning to speak its language. To them, peace and happiness are illegal immigrants trying to invade their realities.

Proverb of Fire 909
Letting the sun set on your wrath is the same as having a sleepover with Satan.

Proverb of Fire 910
A woman who marries a man she doesn't respect is a woman who's estranged from peace.

Proverb of Fire 911
If you marry the wrong man, Satan will be your father-in-law.

Proverb of Fire 912
When a baby comes into this world, it spends a lot of its time crying because the baby has to adjust to this new place. The baby is dependent on the parents and has to be carried around until he or she learns to stand on his or her own. The same goes for you and me. We are often shifted to new places, new realms and new mindsets, and oftentimes, our first response is to cry. We don't understand where we are or how to stand up on our own in these new places, but God will carry us until we adjust to our new settings.

Proverb of Fire 913
Marrying a person who does not fear the Lord is like trying to hug a porcupine.

Proverb of Fire 914
A woman who uses sex to get a man is a woman Satan uses to get a man. In other words, she's bait.

Proverb of Fire 915
God will never allow your God-ordained spouse to propose to you until you've accepted His proposal. Any marriage that's established out of order will operate out of order. Accept the call on your life first, and then, you will be found by the man of God who's accepted the call on his life.

Proverb of Fire 916
The Devil is terrified of a believer who actually believes.

Proverb of Fire 917
A woman who sexes her way to the altar is a woman who will eventually find herself at the altar—alone.

Proverb of Fire 918
We are the temples of the Holy Spirit. Holiness is realizing that your mind is the door to the church, your heart is the doctrine of that church, your tongue is the pastor in the pulpit of that church, and your body is the altar. Whatever you allow in the church will create the doctrine, preach that doctrine, and make sacrifices to the author of that doctrine. Let the Word of God in so you can preach the uncompromising gospel of Jesus Christ.

Proverb of Fire 919
Good sex in a bad marriage is like fine dining in a sewer.

Proverb of Fire 920
It is better to ask a question than to assume the answer.

Proverb of Fire 921
God has to work on you before He can work through you.

Proverb of Fire 922
David didn't defeat Goliath; God did. David was just a vessel who had enough faith for God to work through. You can't defeat your Goliath, but God can. You just need to trust Him enough for Him to work through you.

Proverb of Fire 923
The worst thing you could ever say to Ishmael is "I do." You'll wish you didn't.

Proverb of Fire 924
God speaks and it is so. You exist because He spoke you into existence, and now, your life is a long story being told by your choices and narrated by God. Your choices will decide how your story ends, and the content of your heart will decide what story you choose to tell. Nevertheless, you're still here, so you have the ability to change your story. You can turn your life around because God has not placed a period at the end of your sentence. See your life as a story, and decide how you want it to read. After that, change your story!

Proverb of Fire 925
Common sense will help you climb the mountain, but wisdom will teach you how to move a mountain.

Proverb of Fire 926
Just because it's sitting in the sanctuary doesn't mean it's marriage material. If you don't try the spirit, the spirits (devils) will try you. Don't end up happily engaged only to

find yourself unhappily married.

Proverb of Fire 927
The root word of "discipline" is "disciple." You can't become God's disciple if you're not disciplined.

Proverb of Fire 928
Flesh turns the heads of worldly men, but holiness will get your husband's attention.

Proverb of Fire 929
A man can never rise above his understanding. The width, depth, height, and breadth of a man's understanding is the fuel that determines how far he will go in life. Everything else is just hot air.

Proverb of Fire 930
If you marry an adulterer, don't be surprised when the adulterer does what adulterers do— commit adultery. It's when an adulterer is faithful that you ought to be surprised.

Proverb of Fire 931
Sexy women get sexed, but holy women get married.

Proverb of Fire 932
Man's rejection is oftentimes the result of God's acceptance.

Proverb of Fire 933
Fear freezes the body, but faith moves the soul.

Proverb of Fire 934
Your praise is a perfume that attracts the blessings of God. It is also a devil repellent.

Proverb of Fire 935
Fear is an aphrodisiac for the Devil. If you wear it, you'll turn him on.

Proverb of Fire 936
A jewel that is not hidden is either worthless or lost.

Proverb of Fire 937
Many of us tell stories we should never have had to tell about people we shouldn't have ever known because of situations we shouldn't have put ourselves in. In other words, stop starting fires, and then, complaining when you get burned.

Proverb of Fire 938
Believing in the Word of God and acting out in faith is more than a reflection of who I am, but it is a rejection of who I was.

Proverb of Fire 939
Every storm presents an opportunity to start anew. Choosing to stay put rather than starting afresh means you are choosing to be nothing more than a spiritual ghost town. Move with the winds of change, not against them.

Proverb of Fire 940
The first person you have to correct everyday is yourself. Once you get back in line, you can minister to others who are out of line.

Proverb of Fire 941
One of the keys to getting ahead is to stop looking back.

Proverb of Fire 942
Never sow into a person who refuses to sow into himself or herself.

Proverb of Fire 943
Satan needs a sin offering to successfully attack you.

Proverb of Fire 944
An adulterer is not a person who can be changed; they have to be delivered.

Proverb of Fire 945
So many of us complain about people using us, but there is a solution to this problem. Users are opportunists and opportunists need opportunities. Take away the opportunities and the opportunists will leave.

Proverb of Fire 946
God's amazing grace is the reason we're still here. If God lets sin do to us what it had the rights to do, we'd all be dead or crazy.

Proverb of Fire 947
You are either being distracted by the shadows of your past or the visions of your future. If yesterday has you, today must go on without you.

Proverb of Fire 948
A man of the flesh goes after women who are led by their flesh, but a man of the Spirit seeks to find a woman who is clothed with the garment of holiness. Regardless of what religious title a man holds, you will always know what he is led by based on the type of women he pursues.

Proverb of Fire 949
God presented the Word, and now, we have to represent the Word.

Proverb of Fire 950
If a man has one million dollars, and he spends one dollar out of that million, he is no longer a millionaire. If he sows one dollar of his money into good ground, he is still a millionaire and may become a multimillionaire because he can expect a return on what he's sown. The difference between a rich man and a poor man is what they do with their money. A poor man spends, but a rich man invests. The word "invest" is just the corporate word for "sow." Spent money goes out with a one-way ticket never to return. Seeds sown are sent out with a round trip ticket, and even though they leave you today, they are scheduled to return with more in the near future. How do you go from being a poor man to a rich man? It's simple. You sow your way out.

Proverb of Fire 951
If you haven't offended the Devil, it's because you've flattered him.

Proverb of Fire 952
We are never better than one another; sometimes, we're just better off.

Proverb of Fire 953
Sometimes, the Devil tries to destroy your testimony and accidentally ends up giving you a new one.

Proverb of Fire 954
You attract what you are, so be holy. If you're still wrestling

with perversion, do not seek to be married yet, otherwise, you'll attract a perverted spouse. Seek to be delivered first, and when you become the spouse you want to attract, it is then that you should ask the Lord to review your heart to make sure that you're ready for the one He has for you.

Proverb of Fire 955
You can't get along with someone else if you don't know how to be alone with yourself.

Proverb of Fire 956
If you connect an extension cord to a socket, it's going to draw power from that socket. Anytime you connect with people, the same happens. You will draw power from whatever they are powered by. If they are not in submission to God, you're gonna mess up and draw the wrong type of power.

Proverb of Fire 957
Let's break down the word "idolater." I-do-later. How many of you are serving the enemy, but planning to serve the Lord later?

Proverb of Fire 958
True love is without limits or boundaries, but when folks get married with conditions, they enter marriage without one of the key components of love: grace. Without grace, your marriage cannot survive.

Proverb of Fire 959
Adultery is when you cheat on your spouse; idolatry is when you cheat on God. Every adulterous spouse was first an idolater (they submitted themselves to selfishness, or better

yet, self- worship) before they became an adulterer. The point is—if you are married to an adulterer, you can't convince your spouse to stop cheating on you before they stop cheating on God. You have to submit your complaint to God, and when He delivers them from idolatry, they will automatically be delivered from adultery.

Proverb of Fire 960
If you had to fornicate to get him, wait until you see how much it's gonna cost you to keep him.

Proverb of Fire 961
More than 20% of the soldiers who die in war are the victims of "friendly fire," meaning, someone fighting with them unintentionally killed them, but in today's church, many people intentionally shoot words at each other.

Proverb of Fire 962
Lies are the Devil's charms. Don't wear them around your heart or dangle them from your lips. They're worthless.

Proverb of Fire 963
Love does not balance sin; it destroys it.

Proverb of Fire 964
Devils love to use half naked, seductive women to lure men outside the will of God. But when those women begin to age and the Devil can't use them as much as he once could, he lets bitterness eat them from the inside out. Don't let Satan be your pimp. Cover yourself and be wise, otherwise, you'll be nothing more than devil bait.

Proverb of Fire 965
When I was lost and twisted, I attracted lost men who were also twisted, and then, I had the nerves to complain about them.

Proverb of Fire 966
You don't have the tools to fix the cracks in a broken man's soul. Only God does, but the guy must realize he's broken, and then, seek God for restoration. If you try to fix him, he will break you.

Proverb of Fire 967
Many women can't be found by their God-ordained husbands because they are unknowingly married to someone else. Vows don't join you to a man, sex does.

Proverb of Fire 968
You can deliver your body to the church building, but deliverance doesn't occur until you become the church.

Proverb of Fire 969
A man was formed by God, but he's not ready to be a husband until he's been transformed by God.

Proverb of Fire 970
There is a butterfly referred to as the Monarch butterfly. The Monarch butterfly is toxic because it eats milkweed. They are also bitter-tasting, so most of their predators avoid them and will refuse to eat them. It goes without saying, a bird, for example, may eat a Monarch one time in its life, and after that, it avoids Monarchs altogether. There is another butterfly that looks very similar to the Monarch, and it's called a Viceroy butterfly. Now, a Viceroy isn't poisonous or

bitter at all, but because it looks so much like the Monarch, it's often mistaken for the Monarch and predators avoid it as well. The Monarch's protection is that its toxic and bitter, but the Viceroy's protection is that it looks like the Monarch. Here's a word for you. You look like any other woman; that's God's protection for you. Your husband (if he hasn't found you yet) has gone through his fair share of bitter females and toxic relationships to the point that if he was to see you (in the natural), he'd probably think you were just like the rest of the women he has had in his life. That's where God comes in. You see, a man cannot see a woman's heart, therefore, he'll go by what he does see: his understanding and his fears. But if you stay in the Lord, God will show your husband that you are not a Monarch (bitter woman), but you are the Viceroy (wife) that he's been looking for. If you don't wait on God, you will end up being consumed by the enemy. Please understand that Satan has many ways of consuming a person, and one of his favorite ways to consume a woman is by using the mouth of a man! Satan knows that if he can get you to start trusting in your own devices, and "dating" men, he can hook you up with a few Monarchs. That way, when Mr. Viceroy comes around, you won't know the difference between him and the toxic men you've dated. That's when you'll start trusting in your own eyes, and you'll reject your Viceroy because he looks like a Monarch you once had. Only God can bring together "holy" matrimony for He is holy, and you cannot find holiness outside of Him. You can't be found by looking; you have to be hidden.

Proverb of Fire 971

Die to your flesh before you even consider marriage. Marriage is not a union that will make you whole; instead, marriage is a union that can only be maintained by two whole people. Broken people get married to break up.

Proverb of Fire 972
Yesterday is behind me; tomorrow is inside me, but today walks with me always.

Proverb of Fire 973
Evil communication is like giving Satan your itinerary.

Proverb of Fire 974
If you want to be blessed, you must first learn to be a blessing.

Proverb of Fire 975
Anyone who calls a religious man holy is just as blind as a person who calls a holy man religious.

Proverb of Fire 976
Who you really are and who you've learned to be are two different people.

Proverb of Fire 977
Some people answer their lack while questioning their God.

Proverb of Fire 978
Sometimes, it's good to just intercede for random people. Practice it and you'll find that in interceding for them, you will also simultaneously be interceding for yourself.

Proverb of Fire 979
You go before the Lord and say, "Lord, I need some money to pay these bills of mine. I don't know what I'm going to do!

Lord, I need some patience to deal with these family members of mine! They are running me crazy! Lord, please send me a husband. I'm tired of being lonely!" And the Lord looks at you and all He sees are the seeds you've sown and the harvest you're reaping, so He responds, "Don't you pay to get into the club? Why aren't you calling on them since that's where you're tithing! Why is it that you throw parties for the Devil, and then, call my name when the Devil shows up? Didn't I tell you to distance yourself from those family members, and yet, you ask me to give you the patience to disobey me? Husband? You haven't even committed yourself wholly to me yet. You don't even know what it means to be a wife yet because you have not yet acknowledged me outside of your religiousness!" Here's the thing, people of God. We sow, and then, we reap. We sow again, and then, we reap again. We look at our lives and see the harvest that's growing up, and then, we cry out to God and ask Him for a better harvest, but God answers through seeds! You cannot sow discord and expect to reap a blessing! So, when God hands you a seed, it's up to you whether you will obey Him and sow that seed or if you will consume it! Many of you take the seeds that God has given you, and you sow them into bad ground (clubbing, drinking, smoking, fornicating, rebellious souls). After that, you see the harvest and begin to cry out that the Devil is attacking you. No, he's not! You are reaping what you're sowing! If you do not like what's growing up in your life, repent! After you TRULY repent, take whatever seeds God gives you and do whatever He tells you to do with them. Obey Him and you'll see better harvests!

Proverb of Fire 980
Telling the Devil that he's a liar is nothing more than religious

chanting if you believe him.

Proverb of Fire 981
A man can have a meaningless, long-term sexual relationship, and even temporarily co-exist with a woman he has no intentions or desires to marry. It's called having a roommate with benefits. Don't end up becoming some man's decoy while he waits for a woman worth marrying to come along.

Proverb of Fire 982
Oftentimes, we surrender our lives to the Lord, but we forget to surrender our minds to Him.

Proverb of Fire 983
There's a difference between wisdom and intelligence. Wisdom comes from God and goes against our natural understanding, whereas, intelligence is determined by the world's system. You can be wise and intelligent, but wisdom will always take you further than intelligence.

Proverb of Fire 984
Some people are married to their roadblocks. Don't become one of them.

Proverb of Fire 985
Some of you were born into families that are NOT your families! You were simply being conditioned and trained; you were just passing through! Even though you went through some of the worst hardships known to man, you survived and you found out that no mountain, obstacle, or person had the power or the right to take you out! Instead, after enduring so much, you tapped into a strength that most

people covet. But here's the thing. You have to recognize that those former ties aren't your God-appointed ties, therefore, stop trying to reconcile with folks who want no part of God. They are not your kinsmen! Who are my mother and my brothers? Those who do the will of my Father! Let go of the hindrances, the familiar spirits, the strongmen and be sure to denounce the old mindset because it will try to reapply for a position in your heart. God will give you a family—people who are related to you through the blood of Jesus, and they'll be closer to you than the folks you grew up with. Remember what Christ said. Matthew 10:34-36 (NIV): "Do not suppose that I have come to bring peace to the earth. I did not come to bring peace, but a sword. For I have come to turn a man against his father, a daughter against her mother, a daughter-in-law against her mother-in-law—a man's enemies will be the members of his own household."

Proverb of Fire 986
The best day for your parents was the day you were born; the best day for God was the day you were born again!

Proverb of Fire 987
The enemy puts in overtime trying to make you doubt God, fear him (the devil) and abort your blessings. He looks at the mess he's made and is proud of all the chaos. From underneath the ruin, he hears you—and at first, he thinks you're crying. His smile is short-lived, however, when he realizes you are STILL praising God. But wait! Now fear sets in with him because he hears the host of Heaven joining you in the praise. Just as the devils he's assigned to attack you attempt to flee, you bind them and cast them into the pit (spirit prison) until the day of judgment. Your blessings

overtake you and God is glorified. Make that happen right now. Your sword is in your mouth!

Proverb of Fire 988
Sometimes, a test is not the evidence of an attack. Sometimes, a test is the evidence of the conception of your blessings you have been praying for. Your test is just a positive pregnancy test. Don't abort your blessings just because they are altering your lifestyle. By blessing the name of the Lord and thanking Him in advance, you are in the same way nurturing those blessings and a miracle shall be born to you. Too many people of God pray for change, but when they conceive it, they abort it because they don't like the changes that come with it.

Proverb of Fire 989
You can't get mad at a person for who they are, but you can change their status in your life.

Proverb of Fire 990
If you look up to worldly celebrities, it's only because the world has turned you upside down.

Proverb of Fire 991
Heaven plays Scrabble against hell, and the game is tied with you being the last player on heaven's team. To secure the win, your life right now (Sundays excluded) would have to spell victory. Would heaven win with you, or would you only have enough letters to spell victim?

Proverb of Fire 992
In the game of love, Satan has already lost and that's why you need to stay in love to maintain your victory.

Proverb of Fire 993
There is no safe way to disobey God.

Proverb of Fire 994
A man who is not submitted to God is looking for a woman who's willing to submit to his devils.

Proverb of Fire 995
Sleep is overrated to someone who's stopped dreaming.

Proverb of Fire 996
A man with no vision is a blind man. If you marry him, he will lead you into a ditch.

Proverb of Fire 997
Love is unconditional. If you ask God for your husband and God sees that you have conditions that your husband must follow to stay married to you, He will not release you to be found. Instead, He will take you through a series of events designed to help you elevate above Eros (romantic) love to Agape (godly) love; after all, you need both to remain married. After that, He will teach you to walk in grace by showing you areas of your life where you need grace. However long it takes you to learn these lessons, that's how long it'll take God to release you to be found by your God-appointed husband.

Proverb of Fire 998
We often marry our perceptions of a person, but we divorce their reality.

Proverb of Fire 999
There are many people who've fornicated their way into

marriage and their marriages will last a lifetime. For the majority of them, it's a lifetime of misery.

Proverb of Fire 1000

You don't have to court a man for two years when God's in it, unless He specifically tells you to. All you need is confirmation from heaven and everything else is a green light.

Parables of Fire

Chapter 1

Chapter 1

Parable of Fire 001

Linda meets Joey at a Christian event. Joey believes in God. As a matter of fact, Joey is a preacher. The two hit it off really well, and two years later, Joey finally proposes to Linda. Another woman named Trisha meets a man named Tony. Tony is also a believer who goes to the sanctuary three times a week. Two weeks after meeting Trisha, Tony ends the relationship and the two never speak again. People are celebrating Linda's engagement, but those same people are shaking their heads in dismay at Trisha's track record. She's had three men of God to dump her in less than one year. Linda and Joey marry and four years later, they are going through a bitter divorce. As it turns out, Linda fornicated with Joey to lock him in, but Trisha was driving men away by refusing to sleep with them. Linda had what looked like a blessing, but the tests of time revealed Linda's dirty secret. She had sexed her way into unholy matrimony, but when her vows were tried, she was found to be a liar. When her husband was tried, he was found to be a cheater. Now, the same people who celebrated her are confused. Trisha, on the other hand, has just married a man after God's own heart who goes by the name of Jason. She waited longer than Linda, but she REFUSED to trade in her righteousness to get a man. Trisha's love and fear of God, coupled with her obedience to God finally produces a blessing that will withstand the tests of time. As the years passed, Trisha's vows to her husband were tested, but they did not fail because her love and loyalty had been proven BEFORE she met her husband. Jason's vows were tested and it was found that he loved the Lord so much that his love for God trickled over into his marriage and the love he had for his wife was made perfect through his love and fear of God. Trisha and

Jason go on to have a successful ministry and marriage, and she spends the rest of her life thanking God for the man He sent to her—that same man that God took His precious time to prepare for the woman He decided was worth His best. Will you wait on God or will you end up with a microwave blessing?

Parable of Fire 002

A man created 12 mazes, and held a contest. He allowed 12 men and women (along with their spouses) to go through each maze, and he said that the first couple to finish the maze would win $10,000. People from all over the state showed up, but he carefully picked 12 couples he felt would be perfect for his experiment. The maze would take five hours to complete, and the creator of the maze handed each couple little cards that gave them clues on how to get out of the maze. The husbands' cards had some clues and suggestions, but there were many places in the mazes that their cards didn't cover. The wives' cards had some clues and suggestions, but there were many places in the mazes that their cards didn't cover. Additionally, there was writing on the wall in a few places, and the maze's creator would speak every hour to give each couple a clue. Before the contest started, the maze's creator took the couples out to eat, and he intentionally ignored some couples, while showering other couples with attention. Finally, the time came for the contest, and each couple stood in front of their mazes ready to go. Many of the ones who had been ignored by the creator felt that the game was fixed and had already begun to lose some of their momenta before the game started. Many of the ones who had been showered with attention felt that they were favored, and had already begun to taste their victories and plan their shopping sprees. The game started and each couple ran off into the maze. Within an hour, three couples who felt ignored had already given up. Another three couples who felt favored had begun to feel the pressure too, as they realized that their cards didn't have any special instructions on them. The writing on the walls didn't help too much, and by hour four, some of the couples had even split up. One woman was reading her card thoroughly, and following the instructions, but her husband had become frustrated and decided to go in another direction. He felt that the maze's creator didn't favor them, and he felt that he had intentionally placed them in mazes and given them cards that would mislead them. After arguing with his wife, he decided to go off on his own, while his wife continued to follow the directions. Finally, the fifth hour came, and only one couple stood at the finish line, ready to collect their reward. Many of the couples split up in the maze; some of them gave up while in the maze, while others could still be heard yelling at each other while in the maze. At the end of it all, they all discovered:

1. Every one of them who had been showered with attention at the restaurant had failed. They had become so sure of their win that they didn't put forth their best efforts.

2. By showering them with attention, the maze's creator hadn't shown favor to them; he was simply giving attention to them, thus, ensuring their falls. He wanted to prove that people who feel they've received better starts in life, often lag behind because they believe that life has been rigged to give them the win.

3. The couple who won was one of the couples who had

been ignored. Once they entered the maze, they made up their minds that they wouldn't split up, they would follow the card's rules, look for the writing on the wall, and listen to the creator they thought didn't favor them. They had gotten lost three times while in the maze, but each time, they would put their heads and cards together to see the whole picture.

4. The couples who had split up didn't realize they wouldn't be able to get out without each other, since each one's cards had half of the map on it. By splitting up, they ensured their loss.

5. Some of the women's husbands became frustrated and decided to go their own ways. The mistake of these husbands was that they had left their wives. The mistake of the wives was that they gave up once their husbands left.

Here's the message: Just because you don't feel you were given a fair start, doesn't mean you won't come out a winner. It's the ones who cross the finish lines in their minds first who often find themselves standing on the other side of a loss, but only the couples who remain as one will cross the finished line of faith to claim their victories.

Parable of Fire 003

A woman opens a new restaurant, but she hasn't been getting a lot of business. Anxious and determined to succeed, she decides to host an all-you-can-eat sampler at her restaurant. Customers can come in and sample as much food as they want before deciding whether they want to buy a plate or not. Everyone who comes in eats as much as they can and leaves. At the end of the day, the restaurant owner realizes she has spent over ten thousand dollars to host the sampler, and she only earned $3.50 in return. The next day, her restaurant is packed with hungry folks wanting a free meal. Does she have the right to be angry with the vultures who took advantage of her desperation and lack of patience? No. The same thing goes for a woman in fornication. If you let a man sample you, you're gonna find yourself being sampled by many men, but no one's gonna take you to the altar and take you off the single's market because you didn't value yourself enough to wait. Patience is one of the most important ingredients in your wait. If you don't have patience, you'll have many men who'll join themselves to you (soul tie), but very few who are willing to commit to you. And the ones who are willing to commit can't afford your whole hand; that's why they had to sample you first.

Parable of Fire 004

A married man named Stanley has two guys he refers to as his best friends. One guy's name is Bob and the other friend's name is Steve. Stanley has a newborn baby girl, but he also has a fascination with snakes. Stanley tells Bob that he's thinking about getting a python, and even though Bob knows that it's not a good idea, he says nothing. Instead, he pretends to support his friend's decision. He even plans to go with Stan to pick out the snake. Steve, on the other hand, warns Stan about the dangers of having snakes—especially considering that Stan has a newborn daughter. Steve petitions with Stan to not get the snake. He even goes so far as to warn Stan's wife, hoping she could steer her husband. Stan becomes angry with Steve and ends the friendship. The next day, he and Bob go to the pet store and buy a large python. One day, the snake gets out of its cage and begins to behave like the snake it is. It finds its way into the newborn's room because snakes are attracted to the smell of milk. The snake strangles the baby and Stan and his wife are left to grieve the loss of their child. Bob is there for him every step of the way—even at the funeral. Steve comes to the funeral as well, and offers to help Stan if he needs help. Who was Stan's real friend? Steve, of course! You see, Steve told Stan how to PREVENT the loss of his daughter, but Bob told Stan what he wanted to hear to PREVENT the loss of their friendship. At the end, Stan lost his daughter, but hey—at least, he still had Bob. I know this story is harsh and people don't like the undiluted truth, but it's the only way we can understand the cruelness of sin! Real friends don't let friends dance with the Devil and not tell them that they are going to be burned! It's time to stop playing with folks and just tell them the truth if it'll save their lives or their souls! I'd rather be your enemy and see you in heaven than have you like me, and then, end up in hell.

Parable of Fire 005

A man living in poverty comes across a rich man. The rich man has no wisdom because his wealth is an inheritance and he never took the time to learn what his parents did to earn that wealth. The impoverished man is crafty, so he offers the rich man the opportunity to quadruple his income. He says to the rich man that if he gives him 50% of his wealth, he will use that money to invest in a new idea he has, and the rich man agrees. The poor guy warns the rich man that his idea is illegal, but assures him they won't get caught and they'll make a lot of money off the investment. Excited, the rich guy gives the poor man 50% of his wealth. The poor man runs off with the rich man's money, and the rich man is left without help. He can't call the police because he was investing in something illegal, nor can he sue because there was no contractual agreement involved. The rich man hires a private investigator to look for the once poor man, and the investigator finds the new millionaire. After telling his client the new millionaire's address, the rich guy goes to the man's house to confront him. A fight ensues, and the rich guy is arrested. This is similar to what Satan does to man. You have everything you need on the inside of you, but it's hard to recognize your wealth because YOU DID NOT WORK FOR IT. You inherited the kingdom of God through Christ Jesus. And because you didn't work for it, you find it hard to appreciate it sometimes, so you're always looking for something greater than what you have. The Devil then offers you an opportunity to get the desires of your heart, but he needs you to invest what's on the inside of you (faith) into him, and once you invest that faith in him, you simultaneously give him permission to operate in your life. And what does the devil do? He acts like the Devil and robs you of what you have! And you can't bind him (until you truly repent) because you set him loose! You can't ask God to attack the Devil for you because you have aligned yourself with the Devil. And if you try to retaliate in the flesh without repenting, you're the one who'll end up bound to unforgiveness, wrongful thinking, soul ties, and the like! You are rich! Your Father is the King of kings, and the Lord of Lords! The Devil has absolutely NOTHING to offer you, but if you trust him, you give him the ability to tap into what you have, rob you, attack you, and then, bind you. In other words, you let Satan do to you what God told you to do to Satan.

Parable of Fire 006

A kitten walks up to a man and meows, but he hears a roar. He panics and runs away. A fly buzzes past his head, but he thought he saw an eagle, so he low-crawls to safety. An ant steps on his foot and his mind registers that the ant is as heavy as a Buick, so he screams in pain and calls an ambulance. Isn't he considered "mad"? His mind is obviously playing tricks on him. Such is many of the trials that we face. They are so small, but fear puts us in a mad-like state and causes us to see these things as giants and mountains, when they are not. Anytime you see opposition, something is challenging your new position! Why wouldn't it challenge your old position? Well—why would it? When you're already there. Think about an elevated place like a hill. If you were trying to lose weight and gain muscle, you would lose more weight and gain more muscle going up a hill because of the resistance. Gravity is pulling you in one direction and you're having to use more muscle to oppose that gravity. It's the same in warfare! The more resistance you endure, the more strength it requires for you to overcome and that strength doesn't just leave when the warfare is done. Wisdom is spiritual muscle. In the attack you have two choices: whine and roll downhill—but, please know that you have got to tackle that journey again until you get up that hill. (Just like when your baby was learning to walk and fell down—you didn't let him/her give up—so, your Father isn't accepting that you give up.) Choice number 2: Whatever challenges your position needs to know that your Father's name is written all over you—so step on it and go against the resistance! It'll only make you stronger! Don't be afraid of a kitten! You're only as strong as your faith.

Parable of Fire 007

You have a headache, so you go into your medicine cabinet to grab some Ibuprofen. When you grab the first bottle of Ibuprofen, you notice that there's one pill left, but you need two pills to rid yourself of the headache. You look over and see the new bottle of Ibuprofen; it's the same brand as the one you're holding in your hand. Would you throw away the lone pill from the old bottle just because it wasn't made from the same batch as the pills from the new bottle? No! You'd likely grab that one remaining pill from the old bottle, along with a pill from the new bottle, and you'd take them together. Why? Because they were created to do the same thing. It doesn't matter what batch they came from, they were still created by the same manufacturer to do the same thing. What's the message here? A lot of you go from one unsaved man (or woman) to the next because you think that the one you left was the product of a bad seed, so consequentially, you keep getting with the same devil in a different person. Additionally, you keep getting the same results: a broken heart, an illegal soul tie, and an open door for the enemy. You have to understand that if God isn't in that relationship, that person's purpose in your life is the same purpose the last illegal man (or woman) had. The enemy's attack against you does not change; he only changes the people and the methods he uses to bring about that attack. Satan is the manufacturer of sin, so dating unsaved Tyrone ain't no different than dating religious Roger. If he isn't saved, sanctified, and filled with the Holy Spirit, he's going to be an attack against your identity, your purpose, your peace, and your God-appointed marriage. Remember this: If God didn't send him (or her), chances are, it's the same devil in a different person.

Parable of Fire 008

A guy drives up to you in a fancy car. You like him. Imagine that same guy drives up to you in a beat up old lemon. You don't like him. Now, he's the same guy, only, he's driving a different car. So, did you really like him? No. You liked what you thought he represented, and the idea of how he could improve your life. So, do you deserve that guy? No! Because you can't see past what you want from him. Let's imagine our true relationship with God. He comes up to you in a well put together prophet, and speaks His Word to you, and you receive it with rejoicing. You like that prophet. Now, let's imagine God approaches you in another prophet who wasn't well put together. That man looks as if he has nothing to offer you, so you question his anointing and don't receive his words because you don't like that prophet. Here's what the Lord is saying to the church—You are hypocrites! You say that you love Him, but you surround yourself with people you think will benefit yourself and your ministry! You are vain drawers of men who love the people who you believe will benefit yourself, but you want no part of the souls who have nothing to offer you! Your fruit is made known when someone approaches you who has nothing to give you but gratitude. You will continue to draw souls after yourself, and surround yourself with people like yourself because you don't want to grow wise! You represent your title, but you do not represent the living God! Rather than allowing the Lord to renew your mind, you continue down the same paths, gossiping, slandering and hating your brethren, but yet, you think the gates of heaven will open for you. Liars! No one who hates his or her brethren will enter heaven! No one! You try to justify your "hatred" by calling it "dislike", but if it's not love, it's hatred! Your mouth will spit out every word you speak, and the Lord is going to try you with fire, and prove to the nations what you really are! Lovers of yourselves, lovers of wealth and power, but haters of God's people! You preach, you teach, you shout and you dance, but yet, you have not ministered heaven to His people; you've ministered from the belly of your flesh! Repent now, while you still have time, or you will become a byword to the people of God. You will be nothing more than a parable to the people of God, and your fall will minister the gospel you refused to minister!

Parable of Fire 009

A wealthy woman puts on rags and walks into an alley where there are many homeless people. She's heartbroken and wants to get rid of the diamond ring her ex-lover gave her, but she doesn't want anyone to know that she is rich. After all, she may get robbed, so she dresses like a beggar and heads down the alley. She sees a homeless man sitting next to a pile of old newspapers, and without saying a word, she hands the stranger her diamond ring and walks away. The baffled homeless man looks at the ring and decides he's going to the pawn shop to see what it's worth and how much he could sell it for. The next morning, the homeless man walks into the pawn shop and hands the clerk his new ring. The clerk takes one look at the homeless guy and knows he doesn't know the value of the ring, he likely has no identification and he'll settle for whatever he's given. After assessing the ring, the clerk determines that the ring is worth $40,000, but the homeless man doesn't know this. He looks at the curious beggar and says, "I'll give you five hundred dollars for the ring." The homeless man, knowing that he was likely being duped, says, "That's okay. I'll take it to the pawn shop up the road. I know it's gotta be more valuable than that." He then reaches for the ring, but the clerk then responds with, "Well, it's cubic zirconia. Where did you get this ring? Never mind. It's only worth $1,500, so the most I could give you for her is $1,000. Plus, you have no identification, I'm sure, so I'm pushing it by even accepting this ring from you. The pawn shop up the road won't give you anything without identification. They'll just call the cops." The homeless man suddenly dances with excitement. He's never seen a thousand bucks in his whole life, so he accepts the offer and hurries out of the pawn shop. The clerk, however, puts the ring in his display case, selling it for $30,000. Let's talk about you, woman of God. You keep giving your hand to men who don't know the value of you. You are like that wealthy woman who's been hurt, and because of this pain, you've put on rags and went into some low places, giving away the most valuable possession you have: your soul. And the man you handed your soul to has absolutely no clue as to what you're worth, so he trades you for a woman, lifestyle or thing less valuable than yourself because he thought he was getting something equal to or greater than your value. Now, you have to look at your empty hand and come to a decision: Will you go into another low place and give yourself to a man who doesn't understand your value? Or will you repent to God, heal, and let God position you to be found by the man who knows your worth, and is willing to pay that and more to have your hand? It's totally up to you.

Parable of Fire 010

Someone calls you to say that they are coming to pick you up at seven o'clock, and they are going to take you to the place that you've been wanting to go all of your life. At seven o'clock, you step outside of the side door and wait and wait and wait for them. Everyone always picks you up at the side door, but where is your ride? After waiting for what seems like forever, you head back in now angry with the person. But, the person had pulled up near the front door and they had been parked out there all along. You never took the time to check the front door because again—everyone always picks you up at the side door. Here's the word for you—many of you say that you are waiting on God, but you think He is like everyone else, so you keep going out the wrong door, when He is at the door of your heart waiting to come in. You say that you are waiting on God, but in truth, God is waiting on you! You can't expect to receive the answer to your prayers when you refuse to answer the knock on your heart! Change is necessary! Call God again, and this time, open the door of your heart.

Chapter 2

Parable of Fire 011

You head to the store and find five dollars on the ground. It's exactly what you need to add on to what you already have because you want to buy some junk food. Along the way, you run into a homeless man who asks you for fifty cents to get a cup of coffee. He smells awful and you're afraid that he may be germ-filled, so you shoo him away. You want to keep your five dollar blessing, so you go and buy that junk food along with the other items you intended to buy. Once you arrive home, you feed and kiss your dog and head into the living room to enjoy your junk food and a movie. Suddenly, you're standing before the Lord in Judgment and you are sure that He will let you into heaven. After all, you went to church every Sunday, prayed for people, ministered to people, and you always did a mean foot-works dance when the organist could not contain himself. To your dismay, a screen pulls up and shows you all of the wrongs that you did, instead of all of the rights you did. The last image you see is that homeless man scraping for food while you fed yourself and your dog, but not your brother. As you are watching this screen, suddenly the homeless man turns into an angel and flies up to heaven with your report card. You spoke like a saint, danced like a saint, sang like a saint, but you acted nothing like Jesus! Such is the state of the church today where there are many concerts and not enough evangelism. Don't get caught letting money sit in God's place in your heart. Remember—sometimes, we entertain angels!

Parable of Fire 012

A woman marries a man who's incarcerated. She sees his potential, and she believes she can help him make a full recovery. After all, she knows a lot about his life's story. He told her that he was molested. He told her that his mother wasn't there for him. He told her a lot, and because she knows what she believes no one else knows, she believes she has the keys to free him. She goes to the prison and tries to insert her sympathy into the prison bars that's separating her from the man she's come to love. Nothing happens. She tries to walk past the prison guard—hoping he'll understand that she has the keys to set that man free, but she's arrested. Once she's been released, she goes back to the prison to try one last thing. After being locked up, she's realized that she too can survive in a prison. It just takes some getting used to, and it's obvious that she won't be able to free him—so she decides to move into his cell with him. This is what many believers do. They try to take a man who is incarcerated in sin, and they try to free him because they believe they are the only ones who see the good in him. He just needs a little love; right? Well, the truth is God loved him way before you came along, and if God's love wasn't enough for him, what makes you think you have the keys to release him? You can't free a bound man; you can only go into bondage with him where the two of you will share matching mindsets, matching devils and matching prisons, but no freedom.

Parable of Fire 013

A man stands at the altar waiting as his bride comes down the aisle towards him. He's excited to be marrying her because she's different than all the women he's ever had. Today is a special day for him. Today, he has pulled up his pants because he can't sport a sag in his dress pants. His bride, beautiful and saved, wants him! She chose him instead of waiting on her God-ordained husband, and he's flattered. Nevertheless, he doesn't care about anything else but getting that wedding gown off her. After all, she made him wait, and because she made him wait, he decided to marry her. He's not used to waiting—there must be something special about this woman—there's a mystery to her, and the hunter in him has been awakened. After the wedding and the consummation, he's forced into reality. All that woman wants to do is go to church, pray to God, cook, invite her "holier than thou" friends over, and talk about advancement. Sure, she's a good woman, but she's not right for him. Soon, he finds himself missing that cursing, clubbing, drinking woman who'd punch him if he dared to look at another woman. The wife he has now is always trying to reason with him, and that's irritating to him. To him, she's weak—to her, he's weak-minded—to God, they are unequally yoked. She sees the potential in him to be a saint, but he sees the potential in her to be a sinner, and they spend their marriage playing tug-o-war with one another's salvation. Here's a word for you: There are men who will marry you just because you are different. Men are hunters who appreciate anything that runs from them. It sparks their curiosity and makes them take notice. The wrong man will do the right thing and marry you just because you're different. But once he's hunted you down and brought you home, his interest in you will begin to decline day after day until he can't take being with you anymore. But, when you wait on God for your husband, the hunt never ends. You see, even after you are married, God will continue to awaken the hunter in your husband by putting more in you for him to discover. Because of this, his interest in you won't decline; it'll grow more and more. Marrying a devil won't make him go to heaven.

Parable of Fire 014

A woman is in traffic and she's anxious to get home. She speeds through traffic, cutting others off and almost causing accidents. She's in a hurry because she doesn't want to miss her favorite television show, which, of course, is something that could have waited. Finally, she's pulled over and the officer takes more than thirty-minutes of her time running license plate checks while sitting in his vehicle. He gives her a ticket and sends her on her way. She decides that she still needs to drive faster if she wants to catch the ending of her television show. After all, the area she is now in is not known for heavy police presence, so she steps on the gas and starts speeding again. Another vehicle comes out of nowhere and the hurried driver clips the other car before flipping her own car. A few days later, she wakes up in the hospital. As it turns out, she was in a coma and almost died. She suddenly realizes just how unimportant that show was. After all, none of the actors came to visit her in the hospital, and she almost cost someone else their life—and for what? Here's a word for you: You keep allowing the enemy to make you anxious for your husband to find you. You keep trying to speed through the seasons, and you finally meet some man who seizes the opportunity to take advantage of an anxious you. He has his fun with you, and after a few lies and a few years, he walks away leaving you uncovered. He was the officer who pulled you over and gave you the citation. That was your warning, but you still don't get it. You can't force the hand of God to move faster just because you are anxious. So, you go off speeding through the seasons again, finally colliding with that one man God was trying to keep you away from, but this one is going to be your lesson. You did it. You made it happen, and now, you're about to discover why God